Chunah

Is It the Same Church?

Is It the Same Church?

F. J. Sheed

PFLAUM PRESS  DAYTON, OHIO 1968

The Scripture quotations in this publication from the
Revised Standard Version of the Bible, Copyright 1946
and 1952 by the Division of Christian Education, National
Council of the Churches of Christ in the U.S.A., and used
by permission, are indicated by the mark [rsv].

First published 1968
Sheed and Ward Ltd, 38 Maiden Lane, London, WC2, and Sheed
and Ward Pty Ltd, 95 York Street, Sydney
Copyright © 1968 by F. J. Sheed

Library of Congress Catalog Card Number: 68-55966

Printed in the United States of America

Contents

Introduction
Sunrise or Sunset?   vii

1   Authority and Change   1

2   Authority and Morals   27

3   Contraception   45

4   The Church and Scripture   65

5   Mass and Eucharist   85

6   Ecumenism   113

7   Ecumenism and Our Lady   139

8   How Living Is God?   155

9   How Living Is Christ?   173

10 The Crisis of Faith   183

11 Sunrise or Sunset?   197

Appendix   217

Index   221

Introduction

SUNRISE OR SUNSET?

In 1958 Cardinal Roncalli, whom none of us had ever heard of, became Pope John XXIII. He was an old man; evidently he would not last long. He was not meant to, so we were told by our wisers and betters. He was chosen that the Church might have a short breathing-space, a time to ponder on the problems facing her and plan her course for what was left of the century. Then she could choose a younger man to steer her on the course so carefully planned. On one point these wiser and better men were right. Pope John did not last long. But breathing-space? We've not drawn breath since. Carefully planned or hastily improvised, more changes have come upon the Church in these last ten years than in the preceding four hundred.

Is it still the same Church? In one sense, yes. Christ entrusted His gifts of truth and life to Peter and the Apostles with the instruction to bring them to all men until the end of time. Peter's successor still heads the Church on earth, the hierarchy united with him comes down in unbroken succession of bishops consecrated by bishops ("a succession of unbroken bishops"—I have known two speakers make that slip, I being one of them). It is the same Church, as I am the same person who was born in Sydney so long ago, and baptized in St. Patrick's Church a week later; no other Church is the one Christ founded, as I and no other am the firstborn of John and Mary Sheed.

But a lot has happened to me since they brought me into existence; my sameness includes a whole world of difference; the Church's even more. Am I the same in anything but the physical fact? Is the Church?

Today's Church is made to look even more different than it is by the emergence of what I can only call the Myth of the Pre-conciliar Church. I take three instances:

1 People talk as if the Second Vatican Council had introduced a revolutionary innovation called Conscience. But in fact the Council did not go an inch beyond what I—taught by the Church—had been teaching crowds for forty years. I remember vividly, a lunch-hour meeting in the twenties, on Tower Hill, a few yards from the spot where Thomas More was beheaded. I explained to a questioner that if I came to believe that Christ was no more than a man of deep spiritual genius, I should be bound in conscience to leave the Church and might still find eternal salvation—indeed that my soul might be in more danger inside the Church than out. The questioner said I was lying; the crowd agreed with him. I got it from St. Thomas Aquinas.

2 Again, it is taken for granted that the pre-conciliar Catholic must not suggest faults in Pope

or hierarchy, whereas now, thank God, we know how faulty in teaching and defective in holiness both can be. But in all my teaching years I began my talks on Papal Infallibility with instances of extremely faulty Popes, of whom I could offer a charming variety—including John XXII who, in three sermons from his pulpit at Avignon, gave a teaching about the soul between death and the Resurrection of the body which the Church has had to correct; and Clement V who put the Knights Templar to the torture—in order to save the dead Pope Boniface VIII (whom Dante placed in Hell!) from the vengeance of Philip of France.

The Council lay still in the future when I told a large Catholic audience that the adjuration "Put not your trust in princes" included Princes of the Church—and the presiding Cardinal led the applause. It was about the same time that another Cardinal said to me: "The Catholic Church is the only institution in which a slob like me could be made a prince."

3 I have seen it stated in three recent books by Catholics that one of the great defeats of triumphalism in the last ten years has been the willingness to use the phrase "a Church of sinners," and the firm assertion that "the Holiness of the Church" means the Holiness of Christ. I quote a passage which summarizes the outdoor teaching of Catholic Evidence Guild speakers for the last forty years:

> The holiness of the Church is simply the holiness of Christ. Every member, in contact with Him, has available to him a fount of holiness; there is no limit save our own will to receive

what He has to give. There is no growth, and of course no diminishing. If every one of her members were in a state of grace at a given moment, the Church's holiness would be no greater; if we were all in mortal sin together, it would be no less. The holiness of the Church is not the sum total of the holiness of her members, any more than the wetness of rain is measured by the wetness of all those who have ventured out in it. If the whole population goes out and gets drenched, the rain is no wetter: if everyone stays indoors, the rain is no less wet. The Church is holy because it is Christ living on in the world. *As such*, it is the cause of whatever holiness may be in its members, but its holiness is not measured by their response. Every man must make his own response. The saints have responded totally; and, in their thousands upon thousands, they stand as proof that, in the Church, holiness is to be had for the willing. Every saint is certain evidence that, if you and I are not saints, the choice is wholly our own.

No. The pre-conciliar Church was not a place of muted whispers. Or of closed minds. Between 1914 and the accession of John xxiii the Catholic mind was rather specially alive. Two doctrines emerged from long obscurity—the Church as the Mystical Body of Christ, and the Priesthood of the Laity. Père de la Taille's *Mystery of Faith* meant new and splendid thinking on the Mass (by those who agreed with him and those who did not). In Scripture there was the growing influence of the École Biblique in Jerusalem, Pius xii's *Divino afflante*, the Jerusalem Bible and Knox's notable one-man translation. In Hagiography, in History, in Theology, in Psychology, there was work of high originality— it was a wonderful time to be a publisher. You never knew what the morning's mail would bring in. And authority was benevolent. One heard of occasional unpleasant interventions, but they were not frequent. I remember saying, after one long period of untroubled tranquillity, that if you happened to want to get a book on the Index, you'd have to bribe a Cardinal.

My own feeling is that all the changes ushered in by Pope John XXIII were made possible by the forty years which preceded him. But how fast and furiously they have come. Consider how things would strike a Catholic wrecked in 1957 on a desert island and only just now brought home. His Catholic friends have him in their houses. In all of them he finds the conversation beyond him. It circles, sometimes heatedly, around two words which mean nothing to him—Ecumenism and the Pill. Who in 1957 had even heard the word Ecumenism? Who had known what a handful of scientists were doing about estrogen?

The weeks that follow are full of shocks. The priest facing the congregation takes some getting used to. And Mass in English even more. He remembers arguments with Protestants in which his trump card had been the use of Latin as proof of the Church's Catholicity—"one language everywhere in the world". Then there is Benediction. He used to enjoy Benediction, especially the *O Salutaris* (once he heard it sung to the tune of *Danny Boy*: that had rather tickled him.) But Benediction proves hard to find; and some of his friends tell him that of course it is non-liturgical.

Whichever way he looks, the Catholic world he knew seems to have turned upside down—and so quickly: after all, he was only away ten years. He hears of priests getting married, with other priests performing the ceremony. He hears of nuns in picket-lines, nuns marching with Negroes and communists in Alabama; of seminarians picketing Cardinals, refusing daily Mass, declaring the Pope unfitted for his primacy.

And Protestants. He had known that Protestants need not go to hell—he remembers his surprise when a priest ran into trouble with the ecclesiastical authorities on this very topic. But things seem to have gone far beyond that while he was on his desert island. He learns that when John XXIII died, an Episcopal Church had a requiem in its Cathedral, and a Cardinal sent his Vicar-General to be present at it, and would have been there himself only that he had to be in Rome. And his friends tell him that on their TV set they watched the funeral service for Winston Churchill in an Anglican Cathedral, and not only was a Cardinal in the congregation, but an Apostolic Delegate as well. He remembers when his own Episcopalian grandfather died, and just what the parish priest said when he asked permission to go to the funeral service—that was the first time he had heard the phrase *communicatio in sacris:* he heard it at least twenty times, he was not sure what it meant, but it was unmistakably a mortal sin.

All these changes, we may feel, are on the surface: they need getting used to, that's all! But in the first place the surface is what first meets the eye: and unless the depths are well-known, the surface may be almost all that meets the mind. And in the second place there are changes being talked about which go well below the surface.

Our returned castaway has believed in the Angel of the Annunciation all his life. He is startled to find daily-communicant friends of his who apparently bracket Gabriel with Santa Claus. He quotes against them in the first chapter of St. Luke and receives the biggest shock so far: he is left with a shaken feeling that it is safer not to quote the Gospels at all. And this he finds hard to reconcile with the discovery that Scripture is now considered indispensable. It seems to him as though Scripture had become at once indispensable and incomprehensible. Hardly a sentence means what he used to think it did. Only the most learned can hope to understand Scripture, and even if they agreed, the plain man could not understand what they were saying.

Nor does he get any comfort from what seems to him to be happening to the Church herself. Reading about the Second Vatican Council he gets the impression that the Church was split right down the middle. There were conservatives who thought Pope John a catastrophe; there were liberals who thought Pope Paul a catastrophe. Nobody stopped to tell him how very much on the fringe the matters were about which the Council seemed to be rent in twain—the structure and daily running of the Church, her relation to men of other faiths. In all the excitement he does not realize how much agreement there is between conservatives and liberals upon the great mass of Catholic doctrine which the Council did not feel called upon to treat:

Trinity, Incarnation, Redemption, Sanctifying Grace, the World to Come.

Nor do the mass of Catholics realize it. And to strengthen the feeling that the teaching Church is divided, every week brings news of some revolutionary-sounding denial by some theologian somewhere—and not a sound out of their own hierarchy! Great numbers are feeling a kind of unease not common among Catholics since the lines were drawn after the Reformation.

Yet this is not my principal reason for asking whether we are at a sunrise or a sunset. More troubling still is the evaporation of faith generally. The Catholic Church was not the first to experience it, but it is with her now, especially among the young; once one is aware of it, it is a nightmare. Though Vatican II did not, I think, discuss it, we may wonder if it was not Pope John's most urgent reason for wanting a Council!

That the learned should discuss all questions whatever at their own level is wholly right. The trouble arises when their discussions filter down to less learned but deeply interested Catholics. Between the great original thinkers and the mass of Catholics are the middle men: the writers and lecturers who pass on as much as they themselves have grasped. Some of the middle men are of high competence, some are less well-equipped for this most necessary task; and, as in every other movement, there is a fringe of enthusiasts pushing their own special views as though the Church had already adopted them. There is hardly a doctrine or practice of the Church I have not heard attacked by a priest.

And over all hangs the vast matter of contracep-

tion. A growing number of Catholics are asking if
the Church has any right to teach on morals at all;
and even Catholics whose whole instinct is to accept
the Church's teaching feel that if she changes on
this, however relieved they might be, they will be
left wondering why they should trust her on any
other moral question: how much margin for change
has an infallible teacher?

Pope John opened the window to let in fresh air.
He let in a hurricane. The interested Catholic finds
himself at times not only hanging on to his hat, but
hanging on to his head. Provided he keeps his head,
the experience can be salutary. The storm will
clear, and the voice of the Church will be heard
once more. But a lot is going to happen in between.
I have heard a Jesuit in one country and a Benedictine in another urge that Protestants who prac-
tise their own religion should not be encouraged to
join the Catholic Church—an idea that would
seem to call for a considerable rethinking of the
nature of the Church.

But rethinking means that there has already
been thinking—one who has not thought can hardly
rethink. And too many of us have not thought on
these great matters. That may be why the hurricane
had to blow.

1
Authority and Change

Is it the same Church? Same as what? As asked, it means: Is it the same as the Church we were born into and grew up in, or joined as converts? Certainly it differs in all sorts of ways from the Church of Pius XII, and still more from the Church of Pius IX, as the Church after Trent differed from the one that the Reformers quitted, and that from the Church of Ambrose and Augustine. This is to say nothing of the differences between the Western Church and the Eastern even before the break. Was each a different Church? We must look closer to see what the Church essentially is—if there are changes in that, then indeed it is not the same Church.

1

To begin with, it is instructive to look at the Church as we find it in the New Testament. To a casual reader not of our faith it would never occur that it was the same Church as ours. There were no Cardinals—to start with the most spectacular—and no special clerical dress; no convents, no religious orders. We hear of no observance of Christmas, or Easter, or Lent. Their sermons lacked the two key topics of ours, namely Catholic Schools and the Church Debt—they did not build churches, they met in private houses; and there were no special schools for Catholics for another four or five centuries. Priests and bishops were married men (though a widowed bishop was not to take a second wife). Hierarchy in our sense was in its sketchy beginnings. And only a microscopic proportion of the human race was aware of the Church's existence.

Yet we cannot read the Acts or the Epistles without feeling a total conviction that this is our Church. For all its surface strangeness, we feel profoundly at home in it. The "feel" is unmistakable; if we try to analyze it, certain things thrust into the mind. There is the utter certainty of our Lord's lordship, of the guiding and sanctifying presence of the Holy Spirit. There is the triune God. There is baptism and laying on of hands, with the new life of grace as a present glory. There is the Holy Eucharist. There is but one Church, one visible organization from Pontus to Rome, with today's fragmentation unthinkable. There is the assumption that doctrinal unity is essential. A man who is a heretic (that is, a "picker and chooser") is to be warned, and after that "avoided" (Tit 3:10); "if anyone—an angel from heaven, even I myself—should teach any gospel beside what we have taught, let him be anathema" (a chilling word, but Catholics know it well enough). Paul says this in the opening of a letter to the Galatians.

Sounding through, clear and unmistakable, is the note of authority wielded and accepted. We find it in action upon individuals—for example, in Paul's order to the Church at Corinth to "remove from among them" the man who was living sinfully with his father's wife (1 Cor 5:2) and in his decision to re-admit the man when he repented (2 Cor 2:5–10). Here for good measure he uses the words "I wrote that I might test you and know whether you are obedient in everything." We find it where the whole Church is concerned. When the question arose of how far Gentile converts were bound to observe circumcision and the Mosaic ritual law generally, the Apostles gathered in council (Acts 15), discussed the matter and decided that, apart from a tiny handful of regulations, they were not bound.

Writing off so much of the old Law was startling enough: to many a Jewish Christian it seemed like the end of the world. But the words with which the Apostles issued their decision were more startling still: "It has seemed good to the Holy Spirit and to us." You will search the Old Testament in vain for anything comparable; there was no authority within Judaism that could talk like that. For the first time we see the Church's leaders acting on Christ's commission: "Whatsover you shall bind or loose on earth shall be bound or loosed in heaven."

For the first time, but not the last. Through century after century, that note of confident authority sounded in the Catholic Church. Does it still?

I begin with the question of authority, not because it is the most valuable element in the life of the Church—indeed, it is there solely to protect realities more valuable than itself—but because, with so many Catholics straining at so many leashes, it is most immediately and continuously being called in question.

2

The Catholic has always been assumed to be docile, accustomed to being ordered—under pain of sin—to believe this and not that, to behave thus and not thus. Later we shall discuss what is true in this and the reason for it. For the moment my concern is with the surface, what it looks like to the non-Catholic gazing in. He used to see us as sheep. What he sees now seems to him unbelievable—all over the place the sheep are bleating right back at the shepherds: the observer finds himself wondering if the shepherds have lost their nerve. If this were the real sitution, the Church would certainly not be the same—unnerved shepherds and ungovernable sheep would be something wholly new.

Certainly there is a lot of questioning of authority—by the few certainly; but the voices raised in authority's defense are fewer still, and not nearly so vigorous or so assured. We are seeing what looks like a real crisis of authority in the Church.

Not that voices raised in disapproval are a new thing; they only seem so to those who do not know the history of the Church before the Council of Trent. At the very beginning we have Paul withstanding Peter—withstanding him "to the face"—because, under pressure of a Judaising group in the Church, he had ceased to eat with Gentile converts (Galatians 2:11). And through the centuries we have members of the Church acting on the principle we find stated by Thomas Aquinas: that it is the duty of the inferior to tell the superior if he thinks the superior is acting wrongly.

I am not thinking of rather erratic Catholics like the French King—Philip the Fair, I think—who called Boniface VIII not 'Your Holiness' but 'Your Fatuousness'. We find saints criticizing freely. St. Catherine of Siena, for instance, probably did not slap the face of Gregory X, but he must often have felt as if she had; and St. John Fisher, not long before Henry VIII beheaded him, said in a public sermon: "If the Pope does not reform the Curia, God will."

The change came with the Council of Trent. In the first place there was the tightening of discipline. We have to remember the situation in which the Fathers of Trent had to make their decisions—half of Europe already out of the Church, the earth still rumbling under their feet. There really was a war psychosis. It was a period when theologians were for the first time teaching that the Church had the right not simply to hand heretics over to the State but herself to inflict the death penalty —a "right" which the Church herself has never claimed, and theologians do not now assert. Many of the Council's Canons must be seen as wartime regulations.

And in the second place so many centuries of edifying Popes have affected our perspective—it seems to have affected the perspective of Pius IX, if he really said "I am tradition." Public questioning of Papal action by Catholics almost vanished. Now it is back.

But with a difference. That Catholics should raise questions, concerning even official teachings of the highest authority, is all to the good. But that is not, at the moment, the way they are doing it. They are not putting questions to the Pope, or even arguing with him; they are telling him, as men having authority. We have Catholics writing of the decisions of Vatican II like professors marking examination papers, with C plus the highest mark they can find it intellectually honest to give. (Indeed, after I wrote this, one seminary professor, having left the Church, said that if a student of his had handed in Pope Paul's Encyclical *Mysterium fidei* he'd have failed him.) I get the feeling that the Pope isn't infallible and the Council isn't, but half the Catholics I meet are.

In a few this means a real rejection of the Church as it has been almost from the beginning. In most, I think it is a matter of newness. We have never had any habit of speaking our minds: there is an intoxication in the first experience, and no time to examine so new an activity and to form rational standards for ourselves.

Meanwhile the problem faces us. Our Lord had said to Peter singly (Mt. 16:19) and to the Apostles as a group (Mt. 18:18) that whatsover they should bind or loose on earth, heaven would ratify their decisions. "Bind or loose" was a phrase of the Jewish rabbis; it means to forbid or permit. What is the field in which the Church's authority to forbid or permit is God-given? By what organs within the Church is it to be exercised? Does it include St. Gregory VII's *Dictatus Papae?* or St. Pius V's deposition of Queen Elizabeth I? How far does it apply to morals—contraception, for instance? And what about the Church's teaching that the individual *must* follow his conscience? There is a vast amount of thinking ahead of us.

"Whatsoever" seems not to leave out much. Evidently the commission applies to religion, not to secular matters; but where does the frontier lie? And evidently there is a personal contact of the individual with God which legislation cannot reach; but is the point of contact always clear?

The area of authority includes doctrine and sacraments and morals, following our Lord's "Go, teach all nations, baptizing them—teaching them to observe all things whatsoever I have commanded you." Questions arise here, too, and we shall discuss them—individual questions in each of the three fields, still more the practical question about "teaching": namely, where in the present clamor of voices is the ordinary Catholic to turn for teaching which demands his acceptance?

For the moment let us concentrate upon what is called discipline, the daily running of the Church, the commands and prohibitions issued by Pope or Hierarchy which do not involve infallibility but which we are called upon to obey.

There would be fewer problems for us if only we knew no history. Let us take one example. In 1570 Pope Pius v issued a Bull deposing Queen Elizabeth I, releasing her subjects from their allegiance, in effect declaring the throne of England vacant. One cannot imagine St. Peter declaring Nero deposed, or, to come to a Christian Emperor, Pope Sylvester deposing the Emperor Constantine. The action of Pius v belongs exclusively to one period of the Church's life. In the thirteenth century Innocent III put England under an interdict for five years (Mass forbidden, Sacraments forbidden, to practically everybody) because King John would not accept Stephen Langton as Archbishop of

Canterbury. It was not thinkable that Pius xii might put Spain under an interdict when so many dioceses were left without bishops because General Franco insisted that he must have a part in their nomination.

I cite these incidents as a reminder that there are areas of Church action which are not absolutes—they have become what they are as responses to particular situations, and can change with the situation. There tends to be a marginal period when the situation has changed and the response has not. It was in such a period that Pius v issued his Bull of Deposition. It did no harm to Elizabeth. Its most obvious result was that two or three hundred Catholics were hung, drawn and quartered as traitors. Before taking action the Pope had received the best theological advice at his disposal. Cardinal Bellarmine had assured him of his right to depose. As a matter of minor interest, we note that the Pope and the Cardinal have both been canonized, but so far not one of their martyrs has.

The Bull was not accepted as a matter of course, even by Catholics: a group of English priests protested against it. In the following century, when English Catholics wanted reassurance from Rome that the deposing power was not claimed, there was a surprised denial of any such claim—roughly in terms of, "Whatever put such an idea into your head?"

In large matters and small we find the same story —responses to special situations coming to be seen as if they were divine law, so that any change in them is resisted as a surrender to the powers of darkness. We are living in a period when everything is being re-examined. Upon two questions in particular our minds must be clear: (1) How one is to judge whether a particular practice (not rooted in divine law) is still valuable in a changed world? (2) Who should make the decisions?

3

Let us begin, not with doctrine and the moral law—questions in these areas will come later—but with matters which are clearly the way they are because the Church made them so, and which could consequently be changed by the Church if the change seemed advisable. Here is a list from the top of my head—the things which float into my mind when in rare hours of insomnia I plan what I would do if I were Pope:

(1) The election of the Pope by the Cardinals: this is the present method, but it was not always so. For a long time the clergy of the diocese of Rome chose their own Bishop, with the people sometimes joining in. Cardinals, of course, are the Church's invention and the Pope could cease to appoint any more.

(2) The appointment of all Bishops by Rome.

(3) Clerical celibacy.

(4) The obligation of Sunday Mass.

(5) Diocesan seminaries.

(6) Communion in one kind only.

(7) Reservation of the Blessed Sacrament.

(8) Marriage in the presence of a priest.

(9) Vestments, special clerical dress, various titles and insignia.

(10) Censorship, the Index, Imprimaturs, etc.

I list these not as needing change but as changeable. I know people who would dearly love to see some of them changed, yet would rather prefer to keep others; and those who want particular things changed would not all agree on how to do so. My concern is with two questions: What makes changes desirable? Who is to authorize the changes? Let us begin with the second.

We cannot get far with this question without looking more closely at what the Church's purpose is. We can too easily think of it as existing simply for the spiritual well-being of its members, as an arrangement for ensuring that they shall be able to receive the uttermost nourishment—nourishment of truth and life, in union with Christ. All this is truly so in the Church, but it is *not* why Christ founded it. Its function is to do work in the world that Christ wanted done—to bring His truth and sacramental life to all nations, to every creature until the end of time.

He entrusted this work to men, and not as a token or any kind of fiction. Men were not simply to be spectators at the world's redemption. What human wills and intelligences can do, He wants them to do, with His grace to aid. Any one of us can advance the work, or neglect it, or mar it badly.

Think of the Church as Christ's Mystical Body. The purpose of a body—any body—is not the health of its cells, but the service of the one whose body it is: the cells and their health are a means to that end. If Christ had not needed a body for the work He still had to accomplish in the world, there would have been no point in founding the kind of Church He did.

So we must think of the Church not as a service

station to which we must resort from time to time for a fill-up or repair. It is a society of men with a vast work to accomplish, and in this work every one of us has a part allotted. Unless there is authority, the work must suffer. This is the rule for every society. As the Council puts it: "If the political community is not to be torn to pieces as each man follows his own view, authority is needed" (*Church in Modern World*, §74). Those in charge must have the authority to give orders—commanding certain things, forbidding certain things—the authority to make laws, in fact. And these laws are binding not because the legislators are infallible but because laws are necessary and it is their function to make them. If no law were binding unless it were infallible, no nation could exist, our own or any other. Laws may not always be the wisest or best in the circumstances: it is a sign of immaturity to expect perfection in our rulers and be indignant at not finding it. But unless we feel that to obey would be sin, or that an evil is too great to be borne, we must live within the laws, until the legislators have been induced to change them. Laws would have to be very bad indeed for chaos to be preferable.

There is an area of infallibility in the Church; but life has to be lived, laws have to be made, outside that area. By Christ's decision the authority lies in Pope and Hierarchy. A given Catholic may be almost mad with irritation at their failure to make the changes he sees as so necessary, so urgent, so obvious. We must think carefully about him, especially if we find ourselves feeling as he does.

What makes changes desirable? We feel perhaps that a particular belief, law, rule, practice, is "not in line with modern thinking". This indeed has become a cliché; for many, it is what aggiornamento is all about. We should take a closer look. The thinking dominant at a given time always seems to have a kind of absoluteness: it is the last word, we feel a discomfort in running counter to it. But today will become yesterday, this year will become yesteryear—and where are yesteryear's snows?

That masses of men today find some Catholic doctrine or practice totally unacceptable is a fact to be studied carefully, but of itself proves nothing either way. The bandwagon mentality is death to the mind. Modern thinking must be examined for what is permanently valuable in it just as the Church's way of conducting her life must be. We shall make the effort to do this with the great dogmas and the basic moral principles. For the moment we are discussing not dogma and morals but more surface things, and these often enough are out of line, not with modern thinking, but with modern habits. The question is whether they serve or disserve the purpose for which the Church was brought into existence.

We have already looked at some of them. Yet one further look may be a useful training for the more serious thought we must give to the dogmas and the laws. Some of the things I have in mind were responses to special situations. The situations have changed. Are the responses necessarily out of date? Or may some still have values in them?

The law forbidding cremation, for instance, came at a time when people who believed in life after death buried their dead. Those who did not cremated them. So cremation was held to indicate abandonment of belief in survival, and it was forbidden to

Catholics. All that seems pretty remote now. Yet there may be other arguments against cremation. (I for one want to be buried.)

When Catholics were forbidden to attend Protestant services, the reason—at least in England and Ireland—was quite simple. The Act of Uniformity imposed heavy penalties on English Catholics who did not attend Anglican services, Priests were hung, drawn and quartered for saying Mass; the laws in Ireland added a further refinement—the priest caught in the act of saying Mass could be castrated. Catholic Mass or Protestant service—that was the acid test. Attendance at the service meant that one had broken down under the pressure and apostatized.

That situation no longer exists: the prohibition based on it is under consideration. That we should pray together is wholly desirable. But a service is not only the saying of prayers. If I were a Protestant I should hesitate to go to Mass and watch the elevation of what I regarded as bread being venerated as the body of Christ. Being a Catholic I should hesitate at the thought of a sermon at a Protestant service that might in all sincerity attack what I regard as God's teaching. I should not be happy to have this discordancy in my worship of God.

The necessity, not only for the presence of a priest at the marriage of a Catholic but for any ceremony at all, is barely four hundred years old. Until then, it was sufficient for a man and woman to move in together and announce that they were husband and wife. The State recognized the same procedure. With people living their whole lives in one village, that was adequate; with people moving about more, both Church and State saw that some established procedure and registration were required.

But the presence of the priest, the further conditions attached to a mixed marriage—has the situation vanished which called for these? After all, the mixed-marriage legislation, now being revised by the Pope, is not quite sixty years old in England and the United States. The situation has not notably changed, but another element enters; sixty years of experience has raised the question of the wisdom of the legislation.

In the instances I have given, the reason for the Church's rules are obvious enough. It is not always so. Totally un-obvious to me is the seventeenth-century rule, which was in force for a couple of centuries, excommunicating those who used a missal containing a vernacular translation. And surely beyond the reach of reason altogether was the long insistence that, in those Eastern countries where it was a sign of masculine dignity to keep the head covered and a bare head was a degradation, men must remove hat or turban at Mass!

In Church as in State laws have varied in wisdom: in both Church and State the populace is often ahead of the legislators in seeing the desirability of change. What does the populace do?

4

In the Church as in the State, laws are in force which great numbers of people regard as contrary to the general welfare. There are plenty who think, for instance, that the Church would be better served by a married clergy; who think it a contradiction of Ecumenism, to say nothing of Christian charity, that Catholics should not take part in Protestant services and Protestants should not receive Communion at our altar rails; who think that Sunday Mass should be a matter of free choice, not commanded under pain of sin; who would like to see women ordained to the priesthood and consecrated to the episcopate.

Shortly we shall be discussing profounder matters: teachings to which some find their mind unable to assent or their moral sense crying challenge. But certain principles apply at both levels, and can be seen more clearly at the lower, where intense feeling does not complicate the discussion and the soul's depths are not searched.

What does the citizen do? In the State the answer is plain. We try to bring about changes in the laws we do not like, but meanwhile we obey them: if each man disobeyed laws he personally disapproved, there would be chaos. Consider the commentaries that St. Peter and St. Paul write upon our Lord's injunction "Render unto Caesar the things that are Caesar's." (Mt 22:21)

St. Peter:

Be subject for the Lord's sake to every human institution, whether it be to the emperor as supreme, or to governors as sent by him to punish those who do wrong and to praise those who do right. [1 Pet 2:13–14] (RSV)

St. Paul:

Every soul must be submissive to its lawful superiors; authority comes from God only. The man who opposes authority is a rebel against the ordinance of God. If you would be free from the fear of authority, do right and you shall win its approval; the magistrate is God's minister work-

ing for your good. Only if you do wrong need
you be afraid; it is not for nothing that he wears
the sword; he is God's minister still to inflict
punishment on the wrongdoer. [Rom 13:1–4]

The emperor reigning when they wrote was Nero,
who executed them both. He was a very bad ruler:
he used the sword for evil purposes, including the
removal of Paul's own head. Waiting for the blow,
Paul may well have smiled wryly, as he remembered
what he had written to the Romans about this very
sword: his last thought may well have been: "I was
right, all the same." For authority and the power
to enforce it are essential to life in society. We remind ourselves that the ruler's authority—single
man or group or parliament—does not depend upon his being sinless (Nero was quite manifestly
not), nor upon his being infallibly right, but only
upon his being the proper authority, acting in his
proper sphere. After all, Christ our Lord, with His
"Render to Caesar" knew what Caesar was within so
few days to render to Him. Indeed, He made the
rendering an occasion to say it again; for at the
time He said to the Emperor's magistrate, Pilate,
"You would not have any power against me, unless
it were given you from above."

How much of this applies to the citizen of the
Church? Most of it, I think, but not all. Not the
sword, certainly—though we shall discuss the question of the Church's right to enforce its rules later
(pp. 204–05). But in both societies there is need
for unity, and unity means discipline; without these
it cannot effectually do what it exists to do in relation to those within it or those outside. For Christians, the vast value of unity in this practical order

is shown most spectacularly by its loss. Christ shed His blood for the whole human race, and most of the human race has never heard of Him or His blood. As the Council says, "The Gospel message has not been heard, or has been scarcely heard, by two thousand million human beings"; those who should have taught the world about Him utter messages too discordant.

Indeed, all Christians are coming to see that unity is essential: but there cannot be unity without discipline, and who likes discipline? Only in the Church has "discipline" its full meaning of "discipleship": it comes from the Latin verb "to learn" and can hardly exist where there is no authority to teach.

But unity has for Christ, and therefore for us, a meaning profounder than the practical. He prays "that they all may be one as thou, Father, in me and I in thee, that they also may be one in us, *that the world may believe that thou hast sent me*"; and He pinpoints the unity's essence—one in truth and one in love. Our present fragmentation into different Churches would be unthinkable in heaven: but our Lord is praying for a perfection of unity here and now—"that the world may know that thou hast sent me": not an invisible unity, therefore, in the depths of the soul only. We are to know one another in His unity, know one another as companions in Him, and in His truth, and in the work He wants done.

We have noted that the citizen of the State can work for changes in the laws. Can the citizens of the Church? Not in the same way, certainly. The decisive difference is that in the State whatever authority the rulers exercise resides in the people, whereas in the Church it comes directly from God. Our Lord did not say: "Whatever Caesar shall bind or loose on earth shall be bound or loosed in heaven." In the secular order obedience is a practical necessity; common sense requires it. But in the supernatural order obedience has a sacredness, which includes practicality and common sense but transcends them, as you will see if you give a day or two to meditating on Hebrews 5:8–9: "Although Jesus was Son, he learned *obedience* through what he suffered, and being made perfect He became the source of salvation to all who *obey* Him."

While the Church's laws exist they ought to be obeyed, even if we think they could be improved upon. It is not good for the Church as a whole or for the individual himself that he should act as though they had already been repealed. But the conviction that authority in the Church is essential does not mean satisfaction with things as they are. The Council has laid down the principle that "if the influence of events or of the times has led to deficiencies in conduct, in Church discipline, or even in the formulation of doctrines (which must be carefully distinguished from the deposit of Faith itself) these should be appropriately rectified at the proper time." (*Ecumenism* par. 6)

We should be able to express our views on the desirability of change; people who do not tell bishops the truth as they see it upon matters of real importance—"conduct" and "Church discipline" especially—are sinning not only against charity but against justice.

At present there is no habit of this, no fixed procedure. But the Council has decided that in addition to the "collegiality" of bishops working with the

Pope, there should be a similar collegiality of priests working with their bishop, and of laity with their priest. How far this decision of the Council will become a living, breathing reality only time can tell. It will require two things. At the clerical end there must be a desire to hear; I have met ecclesiastics who were more afraid of the laity than of the Communists. At the layman's end there must be a genuine respect for authority; I read in an instruction for Teachers of the Confraternity of Christian Doctrine in a particular diocese that the views on birth control of Pius XI and Pius XII "were given in good faith." We must not flip Papal teachings aside quite like that.

When such procedures come into being, the individuals or groups who are convinced—rightly or wrongly—that changes which common sense and even common justice indicate are needed in the administration of the Church, they will have a normal way of conveying their ideas. But what should they do meanwhile?

Jumping the gun, acting without waiting for authority, is not the way, not only because Christ gave authority in the Church to the Apostles and their successors, but because there is no surer way of breaking that unity which Christ saw as so important that he was prepared to base on it His claim to the world that the Father had sent Him. There was the priest, in another country, who was so enthusiastic for the priesthood of the laity that, all by himself, he revived an early Church custom and communicants found him thrusting the Host into their hands so that they could give themselves communion. I am expecting any day to read of women persuading some Nestorian bishop in the East to

ordain them to the priesthood and challenging the
Church to do something about it! I have already
heard of lay people, rejecting priests and priesthood
as the Church has them, performing their own
eucharistic services. I have spoken of the Catholic
who may be almost mad with irritation at the
Church's failure to make the changes he sees as so
obvious. Among Catholics who bother to express
themselves, the demands for change in doctrine,
liturgy, morals and discipline are continuous, and
irritation is the dominant note. I have been known
to feel it myself. Let us think about it.

5

What the Church is trying to safeguard is not
human knowledge, discovered by human reflection
upon human experience. It is divine revelation. If
God had not given His revelation, we should not
have it; if He had not given it, it would not be
there for human minds either to develop or distort.
To quote from my book, *God and the Human
Mind:*

> God reveals because He wants men to know the
> truth. For precisely the same reason, God watches
> over its exploration. To reveal, and then leave
> men with nothing but their own best guess as to
> what is contained in His communication, would
> frustrate His purpose in revealing.

He did the revealing through men and He does the
watching-over through men. He entrusted His great
gift of truth to the first leaders of His Church
—they were to teach it always, and He would be

with them. Teaching, of course, does not mean merely repeating accurately word for word. It includes understanding and growing in understanding, unpacking the reality contained in the word, applying the truths revealed to new situations.

From the beginning the minds of Christians were actively at work, bringing hidden values to light, making incredibly ingenious mistakes. The command to teach given by Christ to the Church involved the power and the duty to declare which teachings are not in harmony with the revelation entrusted to her. It would be a poor teacher who could not say, "That is error."

To one who does not believe—or no longer believes—that Christ founded a Church with authority to teach, all talk of authority must be meaningless. But he must face the consequence—that it is not possible to know with any certainty what Christ revealed: we can have such of His words as are recorded, but as to their meaning we are left to make our selection, by guess or wish, among the conflicting meanings that fill the air, meanings uttered by men who have prayed to the Holy Spirit for light.

The reader not expert in Theology could not possibly judge every such view for himself, even if he were an intellectual giant in some other field. Nor indeed does even theological expertise ensure right understanding—the theologians contradict one another in rich variety. They speak patronizingly of protecting the simple Catholic, but the complex Catholic needs protection just as much.

A bishop feels, let us say, that a particular doctrine, true in itself, is certain to mislead his flock— owing to their general lack of instruction or perhaps because of special historical circumstances. And it is a fact of common experience that a statement, true as it is written, may be false as it is read. At the First Vatican Council the bishops decided not to call the Church the "Mystical Body of Christ"—some of them recalled that the term had been used by the Jansenists at the Council of Pistoia.

When a bishop says, "I know my people," we may think he is deluding himself. But he may not be. High ecclesiastics have been known to misuse the word "inopportune," but there is such a thing as "inopportuneness" all the same. Between what certainly is the magisterium's business and what certainly isn't, there is a no-man's land, an area of obscurity. In this area there may be honest differences of judgement as to authority's right to teach or act. Rational men allow for these differences; neurotic men can make an issue of them. You can't be absolutely sure on which side the neurosis may be. One thing you can be sure of is that the neurotic will neither believe in the honesty —nor make allowance for the difficulties—of those who oppose him.

Supposing a Catholic feels that he has made some advance from, or correction of, an accepted doctrinal or scriptural position. Are his human rights infringed if the ecclesiastical authorities won't allow him to teach it? If he accepts the Church's teaching authority in general he will not cancel his acceptance because he feels that a given official is using it stupidly. In any society, Church or State, there is always likely to be a gap between the ablest thinkers in it and the men who have to run it—not only because of the superior intellects of the one sort, not only because study is their life work while the officials have so much else to occupy their minds; but also because the officials have a responsibility that the thinkers have not. They must give new ideas time to prove themselves before committing society to them: geniuses, after all, have been wrong—though not perhaps as often as officials.

Anyhow there is the gap. The brilliant thinker is impatient—he can see it all so clearly. So he accuses the officials of preferring authority to truth. They may, of course—*their* own authority especially. Egoism must always be allowed for—the official exaggerating his own importance, the thinker exaggerating the importance of his discovery. Controversial excitement can deflect judgement as surely as sexual, with the victim equally unconscious of the deflection. But to think that the Church as a whole sacrifices truth to authority is to forget the great mass of truth already there about God and man, about where we came from, where we are meant to be going, how we are to get there. It is authority which has preserved it: with no voice to say what is in accord with Christ's teaching, there would be more than a hint of chaos. Every man would be left to make his own choices, the majority deciding to leave it all alone.

After all, if the new idea really is true, it will come to acceptance. The thinker can still discuss it with his intellectual peers, by word of mouth, or in the periodicals they read. It would be closer to reality to say that, even at its most intransigent, the official Church prefers authority to chaos, even though a newly developing facet of truth may be slowed down. Her slowing down of advance in this or that area must be seen in proportion to the protection of the great mass of truth already developed, from which advance can most surely be made.

The Church in fact has two distinct problems here: to protect the truth, and to protect her members. Is veto the best means of protecting truth? All human experience suggests that the mind develops in freedom. An example immediately to our purpose is the whole series of advances made by Theology in conflict with heresies: if those heresies had never been uttered, Theology would be the poorer. So we thank God for them. Or do we?

Certainly as a general principle, one copes best with error not by muzzling it but by answering it. Unless it is fully uttered it cannot be fully answered. On the other hand, the Catholic needs to know when a given teaching is out of harmony with the truths, doctrinal or moral, entrusted by Christ to His Church. However far the Church may go in the direction of non-interference, this other need will have to be met. Authority can swell into tyranny certainly. But freedom can collapse into muddle. Either way truth suffers.

Obviously the best protection against religious error is to build in the Catholic such a knowledge both of doctrine and of the *meaning* of authority, such an awareness of the living values in the Catholic way, that his whole tendency will be to reject foreign elements. Compared with that, protecting him from hearing error is a poor second best. What's more, it doesn't work. What with radio and television and cinema and daily conversation, such a razzamatazz of ideas come pouring into us all the time that not much is gained by blocking the least-frequented channel—I mean religious books.

My own feeling is that something like the Index

will continue, not for prohibition, but for information. Authors perhaps will be under no obligation to withdraw "indexed" books, readers under no obligation to shun them. But at least if a Catholic chooses to read one, he will have been warned: he will not be misled into thinking he is getting Catholic teaching.

Something of the same sort may happen to the *Imprimatur*—it may function more flexibly than in the past (the writer may be allowed to ask any priest in good standing to act as censor); and there may be no obligation. For myself, I find it a relief to have an *Imprimatur* in the books I have written—the reader doesn't have to take my word for it that I am giving him Catholic doctrine.

Things may work out quite differently, of course. But I think one simple psychological principle is now grasped: to force protection on people who don't want it is not protective.

2
Authority and Morals

For forty years I have had street-corner hecklers
saying that to let the Church decide for us what is
morally right or wrong is moral suicide. Now we
hear Catholic voices saying very much the same
thing. What has suddenly become an issue over-
night is not simply the Church's right to refuse the
sacraments to people who divorce and remarry,
for instance, or practice artificial birth control, but
her right to give us laws at all in the field of morals.
In an extreme form this means that it is for everyone
to apply the general principles of divine Revelation
to each situation as it confronts him. Less extreme
is the view of those who accept Christian morality
as it now stands, but feel that in a given instance it
must be modified, that there are no moral laws—
Christ's or any other—binding in every circumstance.

If the Church came to accept this view even in its
less extreme form, it would really be no longer the
same Church—neither the Church we have grown
up in, nor the Church we find in the New Testament. The documents of the Second Vatican Coun-

27

cil flatly contradict it. We shall come back to this. Meanwhile, let us consider the idea on its merits.

1

Those who urge it even at its farthest stretch are not anarchists; they are not urging moral license. But they want moral questions settled by means other than the teaching authority of the Church—either by the acceptance of the standards developed by human society as it copes with the problems social life sets, or by the application of Christ's two commandments of love to each situation as it arises.

To the former I should not have thought Catholics liable if I had not been reading the lengthy document issued for the guidance of Catholic teachers from which I have already quoted. It makes no reference to the Church as a moral teacher (apart from a gibe at rulers who "alone know what is good for others, especially in areas where they do not have problems"). And it gives a definition of morality as "the attempt on the part of the community to express its faith (culture)."

The community is a most unsafe moral guide because, as we shall see, it lacks certain elements essential for judgement; but, quite apart from that, the history of communities as the guardians of morality is hair-raising. There was Sparta, which made homosexuality the basic social relation, wives being used only for child-bearing. There were the Aztecs knifing the hearts out of thousands of living men in one day as offerings to their god. There were the ancient civilizations of China, so recently exposing girl babies to death by freezing; and Indians burning wives alive on the funeral pyre of their husbands until Britain outlawed the practice. (India's present government outlaws it too, though there are rumours that in remote places it is happening again.) I need not name countries of today in which sexual promiscuity is normal; countries in which political corruption is normal; countries in which political assassination is all but part of the Constitution. And if anyone thinks of his own country as a glowing exception, at least he can hardly deny that its very exceptionalness means that what communities in general do is no guide to moral rightness.

Societies do not rise above the level of their members—societies in fact *are* their members—and their moral codes must be based upon something more profound than their own judgement.

The writer of the document we have been glancing at is an exceptional case. Most of the Catholics who want the Church's authority removed from the field of morals are not thus ignoring Christ or the Church. The Church, they believe, exists to teach salvation in Christ; but they urge that decisions as to what it is right or wrong to do in particular cases must be left to the individual Catholic. The Church's moral teachings are guidelines only. Christ reduced the Commandments to two, love of God, love of our fellow man: these are the absolutes, there are no others.

The great Calvinist, Karl Barth, has said that while adultery is wrong, a case is thinkable in which it would be right to commit it. Under a Catholic signature I read: "Morality is not based on immutable laws"; the question is "What is the Christ-like thing to do?" The Christian must do what love calls him to do, under no compulsion, even from God.

In all this there is a lot of self-deception—I should like some day to write a book on auto-kiddery, and this particular matter would have a long chapter to itself. Man's power to persuade himself that the thing he is aflame with desire to do is the loving thing to do seems to be limitless. For a long time now we have had the maxim that any action is allowable provided it does not hurt other people. We have all known cases in which people have broken their marriages convinced they were hurting no one, blind to the anguish of the other partner and of the children: and naturally with no awareness at all of the harm done to society, whose health is bound up with the stability of family life.

One feels that only people of weak passions, easily controlled, could fail to realize that sexual love can be corroded more easily than any other power, and itself needs the control of law. When the blood is on the boil, men are in no condition to apply the test "What is the Christ-like thing to do?" What they need to know is what Christ has told them to do. They need a physician.

Did Christ mean the Two Commandments as a replacement of the Ten? He had already answered the rich young man who wanted to know what he must do to inherit eternal life: "You know the commandments: 'Do not kill, Do not commit adultery, Do not steal, Do not bear false witness, Do not defraud, Honor your father and mother'" (Mk 10:19 [RSV]). When commenting on the ritual laws on eating and drinking, He said that what went into a man mattered little compared with what came out of him—fornication, murder, theft, adultery, slander, coveting: "These are what defile a man" (Mt 15:10–20). He selected the Two Commandments of love, He stated their relation to God's law as a whole: "There is no other command greater than these" (Mk 12:31): "Upon them depend the whole law and the prophets"—these are not abolished; they are shown as having love as their life principle. Without love, obedience to the commandments is not life-giving. But love is not a substitute for them: "If you love me, keep my commandments" (Jn 14:15). "Going, teach all nations, teaching them to observe all things whatsoever I have commanded you" (Mt 28:20).

The power of an idée fixe is very great. Those who dismiss clearly stated moral laws—Thou shalt, thou shalt not—as legalism, and not according to the mind of Christ, can read the New Testament very strangely. Here is an example, from the Catholic document already twice quoted: "The only thing our Lord condemned absolutely was the excessive legalism of the Pharisees."

The *only* thing? That was not the offense concerning which He said it would be better to hang a millstone round one's neck, or for which He used the phrase, "Depart from Me, ye cursed, into the everlasting fire. . . ."

Not only that: what caused Him to rage against the Pharisees was not their legalism but their hypocrisy. "The scribes and the Pharisees sit on Moses' seat; so practice and observe whatever they tell you, but not what they do, for they *preach but do not practice*" (Mt 23:3 [RSV]). And again, twenty verses farther on, "Woe to you scribes and Pharisees, hypocrites! For you tithe mint and cummin and dill, and have neglected the weightier matters of the law, justice and mercy and faith: these you ought to have done without neglecting the others."

2

If the Church has not authority to lay down the law in the field of morality, but at best to give teachings which the Christian will weigh in coming to his own decisions of right and wrong, how does he decide? by what principles? on what considerations? Leaving religion out, how does any man decide questions of right or wrong conduct?

By a sort of practical good sense, I suppose. His nation or tribe or cult has arrived at certain norms of conduct which sum up its own experience of how life, social and individual, is best lived. And provided no cold calculation of self-interest, no passion grown to a blaze, urges him to break away from the norm, things go on well enough. Well enough? As we have noted, we might consider any given society—the high civilization of Rome as St. Paul described it (Rm 1:24–32), for instance—and wonder if we dare grade it "well enough." But for the moment I am concerned with the principle. If "practical good sense" is all men have, then they must use it. But it is not enough, cannot be enough.

There is too much about life that men cannot know of their own knowledge. The segment of life between conception and death we can see. But why anything exists—including ourselves—we cannot see, or what follows death. If there is a God who tells us *why* He made us, *where* we are supposed to be going, *how* we are to get there, then we have the answers to the essential questions. If there is no

Maker, *or* the Maker has not spoken, *or* we have not heard Him speak, *or* we have concentrated all His utterance into the command to love, then quite simply and literally *we do not know what life is all about*.

But can we not learn to live by our experience of living, our experience of loving Christianity? No, because there is one decisive experience none of us has had: the experience of starting the stage of life which follows death. We have not had it ourselves, nor have we observed it in someone else. How decisive it is, Christ our Lord has told us: "If your hand or foot causes you to sin, cut it off: if your eye causes you to sin, pluck it out. It is better for you *to enter life* maimed or lame or with one eye, than with two hands or two feet or two eyes and be thrown into the eternal fire" (Mat 18:8–9). There is no hint here or anywhere in Scriptures of the feeling—which of us have not had it?—that God loved us too much to impose so heavy a strain on us as obedience to one or other of His commandments would involve.

How well- or ill-equipped is a man for the stage of life he is entering at death? That is the ultimate test of what is best for man, and it is not made under our gaze. That this vital part of the human situation is veiled from us is the supreme weakness of what is now called "situation ethics." The most brilliant moral sytem, constructed without the information only God can give, is brilliant guesswork. And it is to this (among other things) that those ministers of religion are condemning themselves who say that God is dead. They are announcing the non-existence of the one Being who can give us the information without which the conduct of human life is only a series of guesses.

It is equivalent to saying, "We don't know why we are here or where the road leads; let us chart our course." If a man is convinced that there is either no God or no revelation, then he must accept the fact—but he should accept it grimly, with full awareness of what he lacks, not with a happy "Whoops, let's go to it."

So far I have been talking only of the normal rules for living. What of the occasions where not only instinct but even common sense seems to say that the rules of convention, or morality, ought to be broken? When Napoleon had Poland at his mercy and Maria Walewska was told that her country would get better terms if she committed adultery with him, where did her duty lie? Was she to weigh the breach of a single commandment against the well-being of a whole nation?

Take a less extreme example. Two married couples. A loathes life with B, C with D, whereas A and D are crazy for each other, C and B likewise; divorce and remarriage would mean four people happy instead of four miserable.

Take a more extreme case. Six shipwrecked sailors with water and no food; no possibility of rescue for a month: if they would agree to draw lots as to which should be killed and eaten, the majority of them might live, otherwise all must die. Common sense, perhaps, gives a clear-go-ahead in the last two examples, shadowed perhaps by a feeling of nausea in the second. Left to itself, "Love thy neighbour" might easily give the same answers as common sense.

In their answers to both questions, "common

sense" and "love of neighbour" threaten danger to
society as a whole, for society's well-being requires
stable marriage and the holding of life sacred. Does
the breach of the commandment guarantee to the
people concerned the happiness they saw the commandment as barring? No one with any experience
of life would regard that as more than a toss-up.
We have noted the problem of Maria Walewska—
her solution was to commit adultery with Napoleon
in order to secure better treatment for Poland. Did
she secure it? In short order Napoleon was defeated and Poland's fate in other hands. Nothing
that has happened since suggests that Poland's
condition would have been worse if the commandment had been observed.

No one can read the future. No one can know
what will result from the simplest action; the one
thing certain is that the future will surprise. It goes
with mental maturity to build one's life basically
upon doing right, which means observing God's
laws, acting according to our Maker's instructions
for the running of ourselves.

When we can be sure what they are, of course.
We shall be coming to that.

There is a special religious attitude involved here,
a profound difference between those who see this
life as a short story complete in one installment,
and those who see it as the first stage in a story that
will never end. For the first sort, unhappiness here
below is final; they are prepared to do anything to
avoid it. To them the notion appeals that men can
settle moral problems, not by God's commands,
but by applying their own intelligence. In plain
fact this can only be guesswork. The guesses can be
nobler or baser, but the noblest—making the com-

mandment of love, for instance, supply for all the rest—is still a guess. Love means willing what is best for the other: and "best" means what is permanently best, what will bring the other to the next stage of life with the fullness of personality it calls for. And that, to repeat, is not under our gaze.

3

Supposing conscience tells us one thing and the Church another, what are we to do? So far we have not considered conscience. Let us consider it now.

Most of us know the symptoms which tell us that our conscience has gone into action. We have done something or gained something which in itself is wholly pleasurable; yet we feel acute discomfort inside us. For all the pleasure of the thing we did, or all the advantage of the thing we have gained, we find ourselves wishing we hadn't. Analyzing our feeling, we find it to be a conviction that we *ought not* to have acted so.

But what *is* conscience? An inner voice, we say. But whose voice? Our own. It is a judgement that we ourselves make: a man is uncomfortable because his intellect (which is what men judge with) tells him that some action of his was morally wrong —not unwise, not unprofitable, not inaccurate, but unclean: he feels worse as a man for having done it. Note that it must be some action of his own. We meet people who seem to have a highly developed conscience about other people's behavior and edify themselves by beating their neighbors' breasts. But that is not conscience; it is only one special form of self-righteousness. Conscience is the judgement our intellect makes upon things done, or to be done, by ourselves.

As such, it is no more certainly right than any other judgement our intellect makes; neither in this field nor in any other are we infallible. As we look at the nations and the centuries, we find conscience universal, but the actions that stir conscience to protest by no means so universal. Fornication did not trouble the pre-Christian pagan conscience at all—adultery was wrong because it struck at the family, but fornication was simply a matter of individual taste, having no moral significance whatever. There are whole nations, or anyhow large sections in all nations, where this kind of thinking still prevails. As to killing—even if we leave war's slaughter out of account—the mind almost reels at what men have in one place or another regarded as wholly acceptable.

Indeed we see things that seem to us utterly horrible regarded not only as acceptable but as pleasing to God. The Moloch worshipper, for example, would have been seriously troubled in conscience if he had not flung his child into the red-hot bronze of the god's image. The Aztec would have felt that he had not only incurred but deserved divine vengeance if he had not cut the hearts out of a sufficient number of living men.

And there has been so much killing done with untroubled conscience for no reason at all. Planters have shot Indians for sport, colonists have shot Aborigines with no more compunction than other men feel about shooting birds, simply because Indians and Aborigines were not counted as men, because they did not look like the sort of men their killers had grown up among. Only brutes would do either of these things, we say. True enough. But how many civilized men feel the faintest pang about millions of square miles of territory taken from native races by force, or feel any responsibility for the wretched remnant to which the original owners have been reduced?

Men of full seriousness do try to form their own consciences, based upon life as they see it, and to live by it. But looking at the human race, to which after all they belong, they cannot be sure that they also are not likely to make some strange judgements as to what is right and wrong in human conduct. Other men have been conditioned by custom, by the mood of the age, by their own prejudices, by their own interests. No one can safely assume that he alone is exempt from defects so universal.

How much authority, then, has conscience? If it is a judgement of right and wrong, by what was that judgement formed?

Primarily (whether we know it or not) by the laws of right and wrong, the Moral Law, built into us by our Maker—in the sense in which physical and mechanical laws are built into an engine by *its* maker. God did not first make us, then impose laws; He made us according to law. If we misuse an engine it begins to creak, grind, make knocking noises: a disturbed conscience is the equivalent of this when what we misuse is our own self.

The trouble is that we are no longer as God made us. We have been variously distorted by our ancestors, by our own action, by the whole run of human life. We inherit bodies with weaknesses in them; we weaken them further by our own sins. No single one of us has in his nature a faultless copy of God's laws.

Cardinal Newman uses as an analogy the moon

reflected in a lake. When the surface of the lake is still, we get a near-perfect reflection of a circle of golden light. But a wind can ruffle the surface: it is still the moon that is reflected, but only in sparkles and flashes with blackness between. If we want to know what the moon is really like, we must look at the moon; we would get a very odd idea of it if we saw it only in the lake. If we want to know the Moral Law in all its clarity and certainty, to look at our own nature is not sufficient either; we must look at the law in itself, as God has taught it.

The moon, you may think, is rather a long way off—not only in space but in relevance. Let us look at our own body; nothing could be closer than that. The laws of bodily health were built into it as the laws of moral health into our soul. Yet no one of us is a perfect model of how bodies were meant to run. Their spontaneous reactions cannot be a hundred per cent trusted. Damaged by dyspepsia, they find wholesome food intolerable. Paralyzed or anesthetized, they cannot feel the jab of a knife. The spontaneous reactions of our minds cannot be wholly trusted either. They can be similarly damaged by immoral action, so that they reject the good; they can be paralyzed by custom, anesthetised by habits long indulged—"grown practically sightless," says the Council, "as a result of habitual sin" (*Church in the Modern World* par. 16).

Our minds, in fact, are rather like computers. Into the computer is fed a mass of information: it sorts it, balances it, and produces an answer, all in a split second. And the answer is right—but only if all the parts of the machine are in working order *and* the machine has been fed the right information. In our computing minds at any given moment are

the spontaneous reactions of our nature (which may
be a very badly damaged nature indeed, with a
strong tendency to think wishfully), the moral
standards accepted by our society (which are a
mixture of good and bad), such moral teaching as
may have come our way (from our Lord, or Buddha,
or Karl Marx, or from any number of contemporary thinkers who explain away the moral law as
taboo, or conditioning, or what you will).

Let us glance at our bodies once more. God's
laws are built into them, but we go to doctors all
the same; God's laws are built into our souls, but we
go to the Church all the same. And whereas doctors
can only do their best according to the point human
knowledge has reached in their field, the Church
has been entrusted with moral teaching by God
himself. She is to teach men to observe all things
whatever Christ had commanded. "It is her duty
to give utterance to, and authoritatively to teach
that Truth, which is Christ Himself, and also to
declare and confirm by her authority those principles of the moral law which have their origin in
human nature itself" (*Religious Freedom* 14).

This does not mean setting up the Church's
teaching as something distinct from conscience, to
which conscience must yield if it happens to differ.
Conscience is our intellect's judgement of what it is
right for us to do; if we accept the Church, then her
teaching is one of the elements by which the intellect forms its judgement. We must *always* obey this
conscience, for to disobey it would mean doing what
we judge to be wrong. "In all his activity a man is
bound to follow his conscience faithfully" (*Religious
Freedom* 3).

But precisely because we are bound to follow it,

we must take every means of ensuring that its judgement is right: no means is surer than to know what our Maker Himself has said. It needs a vast amount of guidance, and man's Maker is the only sure source of the guidance needed. If we believe that God has spoken clearly on the point, then our judgement must be that He is right. Even if we cannot see it, a clear utterance from God must settle the matter for us; we accept it in darkness and pray for light (which comes surprisingly often from the acceptance).

If only all commands came to us directly from God, conscience would present no problem (though acting in accordance with it still would!). For the most part His will *is* clear—the meaning of our Lord's moral teaching as recorded in the Gospels is much easier to be certain about than the meaning of His doctrinal teaching: and the positive moral teaching of Acts and the Epistles, written under divine inspiration, is luminous, too.

But the Church does not claim inspiration or infallibility for all that she has taught about what is right and wrong in human conduct. In the quotation just given from the Council's Declaration on Religious Freedom, the word is "authority" not "infallibility." Some of the Church's commands are her own application to the human condition of the unchanging principles God has entrusted to her. There can be failure of Church authorities to understand the human condition at a given moment; and there can be changes in the human condition from one age to another. In this field some really wrenching problems arise today when, as the Council noted, "The living conditions of modern men have been so profoundly changed in their social and cultural dimensions that we can speak of a new age in human history, an age in which man has learned a mastery of his material environment which men in the past never dreamed of." Not all the problems are wrenching. A man finds conflict between a particular command of the Church and his own conscience on the matter. The command is not infallible but neither is his conscience. Weighing a fallible utterance of the Church against a fallible utterance of his conscience, his judgement might very well be that the bishops are more likely to be right than himself. And this on two grounds, a higher and a lower. The lower: Our experience tells us that experts are usually right and we wrong, if we happen to differ. The higher: that morals come within the teaching commission given by Christ to His Church. Most of us feel the force of what the Jesuit Father R.A.F. Mac-Kenzie says in an Introduction to the Council's Constitution on Revelation: "The Church's magisterium, however much exposed to human vagaries and mistakes on secondary matters, is preserved from going wrong in essentials by the indwelling presence of Christ's Spirit."

If one's mind works along those lines, then *conscience* judges for acceptance. For myself, I would ordinarily in good conscience teach in the Church's way even if I had taught the other way previously. But situations can arise in which a man's conscience on a given matter is so certain that he cannot accept the teaching of authority. What is he to do? He must follow his conscience. To act against one's conscience means to do what one judges to be wrong; and that *must* be wrong, however wrong one may be in judging as one does.

So taught St. Thomas seven centuries ago. We of the Catholic Evidence Guild have been teaching it for forty years, as I indicated in the Introduction. And the Council states the rights of conscience quite clearly, even if it does not in so many words apply them to our special question. Consider three of its statements: "In all his activity a man is bound to follow his conscience faithfully, in order that he may come to God. . . . He is not to be restrained from acting in accordance with his conscience, *especially* in matters religious" (*Religious Freedom* 3). "Conscience frequently errs from invincible ignorance without losing its dignity" (*The Church Today* 16 par. 3). "Man's dignity demands that we act according to a free and aware choice, personally motivated and prompted from within" (ibid. 17).

Following conscience and acting against some Church ruling might mean being deprived of the Blessed Eucharist. And that could mean anguish. It would not be a reason for leaving the Church: the only reason for belonging to it is the belief that it is Christ's, and it does not cease to be His because its officials have judged wrongly or acted unjustly. The anguish must be borne, must be offered to God, must not turn into bitterness against the authorities. Seeing things as he does, the man has no choice. He must remind himself that the authorities also, seeing things as they do, have no choice. In the tenth century the Mohammedan mystic, Al-Hallaj, about to be crucified by the leaders of his own religion, prayed for "these Thy servants who are gathered to slay me, in zeal for Thy religion and in desire to win Thy favor." The troubled Catholic's belief may be right or wrong, but if his love for the people who have barred him from sacraments is not diminished but increased, then he is suffering not only for his belief but for the Church, and his suffering works for its renewal.

3

Contraception

1

I remember reading the report of a speech in which a leading educator said that young men should be able to discuss their sex mechanism as calmly as the mechanism of their automobile. That degree of detachment sounded improbable: men do not seem to be built that way; excitement is in the very pulse of sex. When the topic discussed is birth control there enters a new element to heat the discussion: the thought of anguish for individuals and starvation for whole peoples. Not to be profoundly moved by the anguish and the starvation disqualifies one from discussing the topic. But to be conscious of nothing else disqualifies as much.

Short of these extremes there is a kind of polemical heat—the heat of the argument—which does no service to compassion or rationality: it misrepresents the opposing view in order to annihilate it. Thus in a generally balanced article, I came upon an angry complaint at all the "hell-fire and damnation" sermons preached against birth control. There is surely exaggeration here. I myself have *never* heard a sermon against birth control (pamphlets,

magazine articles in plenty, but not sermons)—
which does not prove that such sermons have not
been preached, but surely suggests that birth control
could hardly have been attacked so endlessly from
Catholic pulpits.

In the same really excellent article, opposing
arguments were dismissed as "smoke screens"—
that is, uttered with the intention of misleading.
It will be a real gain if we try to bring *all* the elements of the problem into our mental landscape. It
will be a still greater gain if we cleanse ourselves of
the habit of accusing of insincerity those who hold
other views than ours—for instance accusing the
hierarchy of forbidding the use of artificial contraceptives because the prohibition does not affect
them personally.

That the Church is entitled to teach what is
morally right and wrong has been her claim from
that first beginning when her Founder gave her the
command "Teach all nations to observe all things
whatsoever I have commanded you": if she with-
draws the claim she is certainly not the same
Church. She shows no sign of withdrawing it. The
Second Vatican Council affirms it with all clarity
in the Constitution *de Ecclesia*. In matters of faith
and morals Pope and bishops "speak in the name of
Christ, and the faithful are to accept their teaching
and adhere to it with a religious assent."

Does the use of sex come within the Church's
power to teach on morals? Is it a *moral* question, a
question not only of what is wisest, best, most useful,
but of sin or virtue?

Too much discussion is carried on with no apparent awareness of the greatness of the act that
is being discussed. It is unique: no other act within

man's power is the channel for the continuance of human life on this earth, no other act produces something which will endure everlastingly. It is sacred since it is a co-operation with God in the production of a being made in His image, made for everlasting union with Himself. And by God's will the "co-operation" is necessary: if there is no bodily union, no human being will be conceived. There are other human powers whose manner of use is left to the judgement of the individual: but comparisons with them shed small light on how this one is to be used, for no other is comparable. A man is entitled to shave off his beard . . . I have heard that solemnly urged as an argument for contraception.

To speak of procreation as the primary end of marriage may have led to an obscuring of marriage as a completion of the personalities of husband and wife; but in itself it was no cheapening or coarsening of the relation. Procreation is pro-creation, deputy creation, our part in the act by which God brings men into being. To see it as less than splendid is to treat the product—man—as nothing, or as nothing much. To make little of it because practically any couple can accomplish it is the snobbery which makes rarity a value in its own right.

But against the splendor of the procreative power is the ease with which it can be profaned, desecrated, used gluttonously, perverted. We constantly find spiritual people, when they write on marriage, glamorizing the bodily union as though it were invariably spiritual, invariably blissful. In the reality of things it is not invariably either. Any given act can mean disappointment, frustration, even misery.

Yet it is meant to give bliss. G. K. Chesterton reminded us that we should thank God for sex as for wine, by moderation in the use of it. And the warning is necessary. Even in Christian marriage there can be gluttony, the ego dominant, the other party a convenience.

The Church has authority to teach in the field of morals, and there is no section of that field in which God is more involved, in which sin comes easier, in which man is more in need of light, than the sexual.

The Church has from Christ the authority to teach faith and morals. One sometimes gets the feeling that "faith and morals" are inseparables, like Siamese twins—once you've said one you automatically say the other. In fact the teaching of doctrines to be believed and the teaching of moral laws to be obeyed are—not only in the giving *but still more in the accepting*—utterly different mental and psychological processes and must be thought out separately.

We have much more to go upon concerning the teaching of faith. While there are any number of infallible definitions on dogma to show us the area and the limits of the definable and the way the Church goes about its defining, there are no such infallible definitions on morals. Hecklers have often obligingly provided me with a reason—namely that some popes dared not make them because their own lives were so immoral. That was simply fooling. The real reason is that on moral questions there has been such general agreement among the bishops throughout the Church and such general acceptance by the Catholic body, that definitions were not called for.

But there are moral issues today on which agreement is not universal, or not clearly so. And it will be instructive to watch the magisterium, the teaching authority, in operation upon them. The Second Vatican Council has not discussed the *how*, but has shed a certain light upon the *what*: "The authority . . . in defining matters of faith and morals extends as far as the deposit of revelation extends" (*Constitution on the Church*).

A certain light, I say. A difficulty is that the "deposit of revelation" (see pp. 74–77) is nowhere formally set out in Scripture. It was given by Christ our Lord to the Apostles, and by them taught to the first Christians. The inspired writers assume that their readers have already been thus taught it: they write of certain elements in it, where there have been misunderstandings; they linger on certain of the teachings or actions of our Lord which mean most to themselves personally or are especially relevant to their purpose in writing.

Thus there is no formal statement of the deposit as a whole by which we can decide that a given moral or doctrinal matter is not in it and therefore that the magisterium cannot teach on it with authority. But we do find Christ's two "whatsoevers": *Whatsoever* you shall bind or loose on earth (Mat 16:18); teach all nations to observe *whatsoever* I have commanded you (28:19). And these are sufficient to justify our acceptance of the Church's authority to teach *once we are sure that the Church is actually committing herself to its exercise* (we shall come back to this).

Where the necessity arises of applying to new questions the truths originally entrusted to her, how does the Church set about it? No more than the human conscience is the magisterium—the teaching authority—to be thought of as a computer, instantly sounding out, or pounding out, the answer to any question we choose to put. For many, new to these matters, the most stunning single statement made by Vatican II reads: "Nor does it wish to decide those questions which the work of theologians has not yet fully clarified." The Church's teaching is the utterance of a mind and the mind functions with prayer and thinking and study (of Scripture and tradition and the human condition and its own living experience) until it is ready to speak the binding or loosing word. The failure to realize this accounts for the impatience we hear expressed at Pope Paul's delay in issuing his statement on Contraception: his mind may very well be unclear still on certain elements of the problem. Until it is clear he must not speak.

Must the validity of the word (that looses or binds) be logically demonstrable? Surely not. To use a phrase, which can be misused but is evidently true, life is larger than logic. Life is not geometry. We cannot always make a logically watertight case for some of the strongest certainties of our own conscience. When all the evidence has been weighed, there is something in ourselves, an unpinpointable something, a kind of ultimate moral instinct, that gives the final yes or no.

There is something similar in the Church, and its utterance is guaranteed by our Lord's promise to be "with" her—in her teaching as in her baptizing—"all days till the end of the world." It was no idle phrase the Apostles used at the first Council of Jerusalem (Ac 15), "It has seemed good to the Holy Spirit and to us."

What does the Church teach on contraception? How does her teaching measure up against our experience of the fullness of life? What margin is there for change or modification?

2

Up to, say, 1960 it was assumed by everyone, inside the Church and outside, that the Church taught definitively and unchangeably that artificial contraception was a grave sin. Catholics who used it knew that in the eyes of the Church they were sinning and that they must not receive the Blessed Eucharist until they repented of the use and abandoned it. Now there are voices all about us raised in question, not only of the prohibition's rightness, but of whether the Church can actually be said to have taught it. The Pope has promised an authoritative statement, but not as though it were something already existent and just wanting to be uttered: he established a commission of theologians, scientists of various sorts, and plain married people to report its views to him. The issue is not as clear as Catholics all thought it was a few years ago.

I am not proposing to settle the rights and wrongs of the question: I have views, but they are of no more authority than any other man's. I have shown why the Church has authority to teach upon contraception. We proceed to consider what the Church has in fact taught—meaning by the Church the *magisterium*, the Church as authorized by Christ to teach in His name.

Theologians can write their views, as can bishops individually and in groups, without engaging the Church's responsibility for what they teach. That responsibility is fully engaged when the magisterium—the Pope defining by himself, or the Hierarchy of the whole Church acting with him—formally issues a teaching or command *as being of divine revelation, or issuing from it.*

"Fully engaged," I say. There are two levels of responsibility falling short of this fullness, yet real all the same.

The first level is when a view is taken for granted by Catholics generally, and the magisterium does not correct it. Thus until quite recently it was assumed by most Catholics that all pagans were damned, and even (by great numbers) that all Protestants were. Only the rare Catholic, of course, would have said that a man who died loving God must go to hell if he did not belong to the Church: it was rather that people just did not advert to the possibility of men outside the Church loving God; psychology hadn't gone deep enough. We can fairly say the Church might be held responsible for Catholics holding the view, since they thought this was the Church's teaching. Pope and hierarchy knew they thought it, and simply left them thinking it. When the Church got around to teaching on the matter, she taught otherwise. Apply this to the question of contraception, and the answer is not in doubt: for the whole of the Church's existence, she taught, at this first level of engagement of responsibility, that artificial contraception was gravely sinful.

The second level involves more active engagement—when, short of formally teaching, the magisterium assumes a certain view as a matter of course, applies it in legislative acts and in the daily running of the Church. To evaluate this accurately would require a vast knowledge of Church history. But at least we can say that the degree of her engagement is not the same when, for instance, she forbids priests (of the Latin Rite but not of the Eastern Rites) to marry; forbids the eating of meat on Friday (but not everywhere and perhaps, in the near future, not anywhere); forbids the reading of certain books named on a list that most Catholics have never seen and would not know how to obtain; forbids the reception of the Eucharist by people in a state of mortal sin; and declares bigamy, homosexuality, blasphemy, calumny and adultery gravely sinful.

In what I have called the daily running of the Church, the popes are men, not divinely inspired, not protected by infallibility. Many a papal law is now seen as a reaction to a situation insufficiently explored. In the Bull *Effraenatam* (1588) Sixtus V declared death the penalty for the use of contraceptives—this was repealed within a couple of years by his successor Gregory XIV. In the Bull *Ad Extirpandam* (1250) Innocent IV introduced torture into the Inquisition procedure although the use of torture had been condemned in the strongest terms four hundred years earlier by Pope Nicholas I. Nor did we have to wait for the Council's Declaration on Religious Liberty to know that any sort of religious coercion is indefensible. Innocent's ruling is unthinkable now. But where a particular line of command or prohibition is repeated century after century with no legislation ever running in the other direction, then the Church's commitment must be seen as close to overwhelming.

The commitment is complete when there is an infallible declaration by Pope or Council—the infallibility having its source not in them, but in God who sees to it that the Church will not be taught error concerning His revelation. To be held as infallible, a teaching must be clearly issued as defining a truth of revelation for the acceptance of the whole Church. Vatican II says of its own statement that they "are not to be regarded as infallible definitions, unless clearly and specifically proposed as such" (*The Church*, addenda).

Only then is the Church's commitment, of itself and its Founder, complete. And this is not a matter of attaching unreal importance to a mere formality. The formal definition has an importance special to itself, for two reasons in particular: the whole mind of the magisterium has been given to the question of whether this in fact *belongs to divine revelation;* and there is a clearness about the nature and the limits of what is being taught.

Yet a historical examination might show that a particular teaching had not at any time been explicitly thought of as involved in Christ's teaching, but had always been seen as so obviously right that the question did not arise. If so, it could be changed not only by stating that it is not of divine revelation but by showing that as men and things have developed, it is no longer obviously right!

Upon contraception there is no infallible pronouncement, but there has been an unvarying stream of legislation, based on a single affirmation about the marriage act.

Not only has there been no infallible pronouncement on Contraception but until 1930, when Pius xi issued *Casti Connubii*, there was nothing that even might be thought to be one. Fifty years earlier, Leo xiii had issued *Arcanum Divinae Sapientiae,* a full-length encyclical on Marriage, without mentioning Contraception. Yet theologians, canon lawyers, and moralists had been concerned with the question at least for the fifteen hundred years from St. Augustine onwards. Popes might utter their own views as private theologians, or approve the legislative decrees of Roman Congregations. But it looks as if the magisterium felt that it was not yet ready to make the decisive, definitive, defining statement.

We have noted that the Second Vatican Council says that the Church "does not wish to define those questions which the work of theologians has not yet fully clarified." The magisterium is growing in its understanding of the realities committed to the Apostles by our Lord, and also in its understanding of the human condition to which these must be applied: "growing to the fullness of the stature of the perfect man" (Eph 4:13) does not exclude growing mentally. When the present Pope decided to issue a statement on contraception, he set up a consultative Commission with laymen in the majority. Although the Commission reported a year ago, he is not yet ready to issue his own decision.

But the Church does not teach with authority only by infallible definitions. What do we learn from the great mass of thinking and decreeing in the centuries preceding *Casti Connubii?* From Scripture the Church did not get much direct help on the matter. The Old Testament has only the story of Onan (Genesis 38:10) who resorted to what was long called onanism and is now called *coitus interruptus,* and was slain by God—apparently for that, but maybe, as some argue, for his contempt of the levirate law. According to this law a widow left childless was entitled to call upon her husband's brother to unite bodily with her to bring forth a child and might—publicly and ritually, so to speak —spit in his face if he refused (Dt 25:5-10). This and the first ten verses of Genesis 38 make interesting reading.

In the New Testament there is condemnation of unnatural use of sex, of the homosexual sort for instance, and the incestuous, and of use outside marriage. But there is nothing on contraception, although it was already eating into, and would ultimately eat away, the Roman Empire.

The first Christian writers to treat the subject applied the Stoic teaching, which linked the act very strictly with procreation. That link has remained as a principle, but the application of the principle has varied from a teaching that makes intercourse mortally sinful if not for the purpose of procreation; to one which treats it as either venially sinful or not sinful at all; or wholly right, provided nothing is done positively to prevent generation.

During the Christian era direct prevention of generation has never been seen as other than sinful, though the attempts to provide a reason for the prohibition have varied. The whole subject is too vast even for summary in the space of these chapters. But two points seem worth emphasising.

The first is that for the greater part of the period biological knowledge of the nature of generation was primitive—certain things could not have been taught if great theologians had known as much as modern school children.

The second is that, while Christian love was seen as an element in marriage, only recently has it come to be seen as an element of the bodily union in marriage. I do not mean only that churchmen did not see it so; it was hardly in men's minds at all. Therefore theologians, canonists, and moralists saw the only motives as either desire for children, or what was primly called the allaying of concupiscence, or more bluntly, venereal pleasure. That it might both express love within marriage and increase it has been for churchmen—as for our whole society—a revolutionary modern discovery. One result has been the disappearance of the age-old question whether pleasure felt in the union by husband and wife was seriously sinful or only venially.

What in sum has the Church actually taught on the subject? One thing only is constant, unvarying, along with all the changes of emphasis, namely, that if the act takes place it must take place in its integrity, complete and unmutilated. When we get the first full and formal statement by a Pope—Pius XI's *Casti Connubi*—this is what it teaches. The act is unique, sacred: it is God's own provision for the continuance of the human race. As such it is the only action within human power from which issue immortal living beings, made in God's image. It must be performed only in its integrity. In the simplicity of that statement of the law we find the answer to a dozen questions arising from the belief that the Church demands procreation at all costs, in limitless quantity. What she demands is that an act which goes to the very root of human life should be performed in its fullness or not at all.

What does destroy the integrity of the act? *Casti Connubii* was directed against interference with the act in itself—the question of the Pill had not yet

arisen. It seems at least probable that the teaching
we await from Paul VI—it may indeed have been
delivered between the writing of these lines and
their publication—will treat mainly of the question
with which this paragraph opens: What does destroy
the integrity of the act?

Catholics are sometimes asked, almost contemptuously, if they believe some doctrine simply because the Church teaches it. There is usually more
reason than that; yet that would suffice. Christ did
not give the Church authority to teach in His name
things we could just as well settle for ourselves.
There are truths for which human vision and human authority are not sufficient even when to us
they seem so. When the Church does solemnly and
formally affirm that a given truth or line of conduct
is of divine revelation—explicitly contained in it or
issuing from it—we may not see the rightness or the
grounds of the affirmation. But we accept. As we
have noted, men cannot always give—even to
themselves—a logical demonstration of their own
most absolute certainties. There is a depth in themselves where the final yes or no is uttered. There is a
similar depth in the Church's mind, and with its
yes or no Christ has promised to be all days, until
the world ends.

As we have seen, not every utterance of the
Church comes from that depth. She does not, to put
it crudely, commit either God or herself equally
concerning the non-use of sex outside marriage
and the non-use of meat on Friday. Upon the use
of sex God has made the whole of human life depend; has made His own creative act follow on it.
He has willed that unless men and women unite in

a particular way no further men and women will be brought by Him into existence. The act of union "affects" Him in a way no other human act does. Through His Church He gives us instructions for its use. And one of them is that it must not be used at all save in its integrity, in its completeness. That is basic to whatever the Church has taught on contraception.

The act may be used at times when generation is not possible; it may be used by husbands and wives past the age for begetting or bearing. Such uses are permissible provided that the act is fully and completely itself. When our Lady was told of the Child she was to bear, she asked *how*. So may we also ask how, regarding this teaching of the Church— how, above all, does it square with the teaching that marriage is for child-bearing? Pause upon this.

There has been a growing volume of discussion whether child-bearing is to be called the primary purpose of marriage, with other purposes secondary. Vatican II's *Church in the Modern World* has balanced procreation and the development of personality in husband and wife to the general satisfaction. But had the question been about the primary purpose not of Marriage but of sex, the answer would have had to be different. The sexual mechanism is for child-bearing as the heart is for the circulation of the blood and the lungs are for breathing. When we say that child-bearing is the primary purpose of sex, we are not merely choosing one use of the sexual powers which seems to us of special importance. We are reminding ourselves that if the human race had not been meant to reproduce itself, the marvellously intricate and interworking mechanisms of sex would not be there at all.

Child-bearing, though the primary purpose of sex, is not—not so obviously anyhow—the primary purpose of *Marriage*. Men and women can marry because they want each other, and the relation can be and often is rich, satisfying, and maturing even where no children are possible. It would be truer to say not that Marriage demands procreation but that procreation demands Marriage—the children require the stable permanent framework which only Marriage supplies. That is why, by God's law, sex is not to be used outside Marriage.

Within Marriage the Church teaches that sex need not "intend" procreation. I don't see how we could be certain about this if it did not. It was an epoch-making moment when Pius xii expressed the hope that science would develop a sufficiently secure basis for the rhythm method. But the test is the integrity of the act which God has made a channel of life. Used as it should be, it still serves the children who are born, or will be born, by making the marriage a stronger, warmer, more loving reality.

To repeat: I have not been proposing to solve the problem of Contraception, but only to show why the Church is entitled to teach on it, what she has so far taught, and certain major elements which she must be expected to take into account in any future teaching. I have concentrated on elements which tend to be overlooked. There are other factors —dangers to the wife's health from further child-bearing; to the psychological health of both and to the vitality of the marriage from enforced abstinence; to the family's economic well-being; to the world's food supply. But about these discussions fill the air. No one is likely to overlook them.

3

I have lingered on the matter of Contraception because it touches the question of the Church's health, and even survival, in so many ways. Within the Church, and in relation to the world outside, it has suddenly become the most pressing, the most tense, of all questions facing the Church. It had been thought that the discovery and spread of rhythm might ease the tension. For individuals it has; but for Catholics as a whole it has not. There is no measuring the results, good or ill or a mixture of both, which may follow Pope Paul's decision—unless, of course, the so-called scientific breakthrough happens which will make Contraception unimportant.

The law against artificial Contraception looms as a larger obstacle to Ecumenism than any doctrinal or liturgical difference. A Catholic bishop told me of a conversation he had just been having with an Episcopalian bishop, in which Contraception was the one matter on which there was no hope of agreement—unless the Church changes her teaching.

But it is the effects within the Church itself which concern us most closely. If the laws as they now stand are modified, to vast numbers of Catholics it will seem that the Church is eating her words. The question will arise: why should they trust her moral teaching on any other topic—why go on accepting the words she has *not* eaten? Why may she not eat them too? There would surely be a crisis of trust.

Yet there should be no such crisis if Catholics have been carefully taught what the definition of Infallibility covers and what Infallibility actually is. If the Papal pronouncement does make—or even seems to make—any reversal of the existent teaching, then it will need to be supported by a clearer official statement than we have yet heard of how Infallibility functions. Without lucidity on this, trust *must* be dimmed.

On the other hand there may be no change. The laws may be reaffirmed in all their starkness, so that those who practice Contraception are barred from Communion (that being, I think, what inflames the whole question.) If so, there will be for vast numbers a crisis of obedience. In the past, when Catholics felt constrained to practice birth-control, they realized that they were breaking the law, hoped God would make allowance, and waited for the menopause to set them free to go once more to the sacraments.

But in one sense, certainly, we are living in a new Church—the relation between the clergy and the laity is not altogether what it was. The priest really used to be seen as a man apart, an *alter Christus*. We might know him well or ill, admire him more or less, but there was an awareness of the sacramental reality which was his and not ours. We might complain of our clergy with various degrees of vigor. But we were conscious of two things concerning even the least admirable of them. The first was that they gave us the Mass and the Sacraments, a service so great and life-giving that their faults could not be measured on the same scale. The second, that until they chose to become priests they were under no obligation to serve us thus—they were not the hired help, they need not have become priests. The priestly life was not so very attractive, otherwise there would not be such a world shortage of priests. That was the way priests were seen, in the English-speaking world at least. That way of seeing has not vanished, but in many it has grown pretty dim.

We find the change in small matters. More lay people call priests by their Christian names (after thirty years I still remember how startled I was to hear a Catholic woman call a Cardinal Pat). Recently a girl told me that she and her friends had decided never to kiss a bishop's ring (a decision which most of the bishops I know would welcome with relief). But there is already in evidence a larger change, caused unintentionally by the Council.

It is one special result of springing the New Theology on a Catholic body which had not been properly taught the Old.

It was for great numbers of Catholics a shattering experience to learn that the bishops were divided—indeed, if the journalists were to be believed, bitterly divided. It was one thing to accept decisions issuing from the successors of the Apostles in all the majesty of their oneness. It was not at all the same thing when the decisions were arrived at by a majority, after—if the journalists were to be believed—lobbying and recriminations not unlike those of politicians anywhere.

The effect of all this is to make the old unquestioning acceptance a great deal harder, especially in a matter like Contraception which can affect people continually, immediately, sometimes agonizingly, as doctrinal teachings do not. Any who are not convinced by the Pope's utterance on it may feel that their personal decision is for their own conscience to make. And while the Second Vatican Council speaks most lucidly upon the rights of men outside the Church to follow their conscience, I have not found that it discusses the relation of the *Catholic* conscience to her own teachings or commands if it feels them contrary to it.

A few years back I was at an International Catholic Congress. It was concerned with two Dialogues—between the Clergy and the Laity, between the Church and the World. My own small contribution was to say that the Dialogue between the Clergy and the Laity was a monologue, that between the Church and the World a silence.

The troubled situation I have been describing— the crisis of trust and the crisis of obedience— need not be permanent. The old relation between clergy and laity has cracked. The new has not been established. In genuine dialogue between clergy and an instructed laity the new relation could come into being, with trust and obedience stronger and richer for being based on Christ's will seen clearer.

4

The Church
and Scripture

"Without Biblical theology, dogmatic theology becomes sterile," says Pope Pius XII in the Encyclical *Humani Generis*. In my judgement that is the most surprising single thing a Pope has said in this century. In all the Church's long history it would be hard to find any official statement about Scripture to match it, or even approach it. One wonders whether the Protestant reader or the Catholic would be more startled by it.

The one regarded the Bible as a Protestant book, a sort of albatross around the Pope's neck, which he could neither get rid of nor live happily with. The other only too often thought of it as an extra —an inspired extra indeed but dispensable; the Church had it all! The Bible was not a necessity of life but a luxury—a luxury in which he himself was not frequently moved to indulge. And suddenly both hear the explosive word "sterile". What this new Papal emphasis on Scripture may mean to the Protestant we shall consider later. For the present we try to see what difference it may make to the Catholic to learn that there is a sterility which only Scripture can cure.

Even those Catholics who were already Scripture readers had not all seen it quite like that. They must look at it with a new eye. What of those who were not? Will they become so? Into my mind floats an incident of my far boyhood. To understand it, remember that I was never at a Catholic school. One day the master in charge of the class asked us what was our favorite book. Every hand went up. We had had the question many a time before. We all knew the answer. The boy he pointed to gave it: "The Bible, sir." The master called him out and caned him—for telling a lie. My small self learned at that moment the value of realism about religion. Let us practice it now.

There is no great likelihood of the great majority of Catholics, any more than the great majority of Protestants, acquiring the habit of reading Scripture. Most people today, whatever their religion, are not much given to serious reading: they prefer pastime reading, pass-time reading, kill-time reading, reading that calls for no effort. Serious reading, strengthening and enriching the mind, they don't do; for practical purposes they can't. They haven't the taste for it, they haven't the muscles for it. And that is the kind of reading Scripture is. Only more so.

We used to be reminded on our outdoor platforms that the Church commands Friday abstinence but does not command Scripture reading—which proved, said our hecklers, that the Church thought going without meat on Friday more important than reading the inspired word of God. But a command to read would have been meaningless to too many people—vast numbers cannot read at all; and of those who can, vast numbers cannot read with any profit. There may be other ways of conveying Scripture to them: it was done, long ago, by painting and sculpture and mystery plays. It may yet be done on the grand scale by television. But by most Catholics, by most Christians, Scripture will not be very much read. There will be Scripture classes in Catholic schools: let us hope they will be more effective than the Doctrine classes have been. The test must always be what remains in the mind and the mental habits ten years after school.

It would be unrealistic to hope that great numbers will build Scripture reading into their religious lives. What difference will it make to those who do? To a great extent it will depend on what guidance they get. The Bible, remember, is not a single book, written at a given time and place. As we have it, it is made up of over seventy individual books, written in various places at various times over a thousand years—roughly 900 B.C. to roughly A.D. 100—embodying material that goes back a further five centuries. The books contain history, law, doctrine, prophecy, liturgy, poetry, drama, parable; they were written in different languages and at different levels of civilization; they require for their full understanding a knowledge of long-forgotten happenings, of long-vanished habits, customs, laws, ways of life. Again and again we find that the scholars have produced new explanations of texts we have taken for granted all our lives. How can you and I judge them?

There is not only new scholarship but religious

controversy. For centuries the Bible has been used as a weapon of war. Protestants have used it against belief in the Church; unbelievers like Tom Paine and Mark Twain have used it against belief in God. And all this has brought in interpretations bewildering in their variety, every one of them convincing until we read the next. Guidance in reading Scripture we must indeed have. Our concern is with what Scripture can do for those who accept the Church as guide.

2

Scripture, we said, has been used by non-Catholics against belief in the Church, by unbelievers against belief in God. The Catholic, I think, will find more difficulties of the second sort than the first, mainly in the Old Testament. If he begins with Genesis he is faced with what reads like a flat contradiction of elementary geology, to say nothing of the seeming exclusion of evolution. This is less of a problem than it was when Darwin's theory was first made public. I shall not linger on it here; there can hardly be a Catholic in the Western world who has not heard it discussed, in school or in mission sermons.

The real difficulties lie in ambush as he plods onward, through Leviticus (where so many an earnest effort to read the Bible from cover to cover has come to a stop), on to Numbers and Joshua and Judges. He knows weariness of head, for this is not the kind of reading he is in the habit of using for entertainment. He finds himself asking "Why am I reading this, anyway?" Because, he is told, it is written under the inspiration of God. But who says so? He goes on from book to book hoping to find God's inspiration of the writing asserted. He reads of God as commanding certain things to be done or said, but not of God as inspiring anyone to write a book. It is from the Church that he gets this. And along with it the Church explains what Inspiration means—that God sees to it that the writers write what God wants written.

But that very fact brings with it a trouble in the heart worse than any weariness of head; for he comes upon cold-blooded massacres carried out, it would seem, by God's command. Upon all this the Church and her scholars have much to say, far too much even to be summarized here. I examine it in *God and the Human Mind*.[1] Every Scripture reader must come to terms with this problem; it is suddenly thrust upon us as the emergence of Salvation History brings us to a closer study of the Old Testament. Basic to it lies the simple truth that the Old Testament is the story of the education—the bringing towards maturity—of a people chosen by God for a unique mission. At the beginning of their education they were primitive. At every point in it they were capable of resistance to God's will, stubbornly following their own.

Morally as well as intellectually their beginnings were primitive. After the moving story of Jacob's love for Rachel and the fourteen years he labored to win her, it is an anti-climax to discover that she is the mother of only two of his sons; the other ten were born of three other women. Polygamy and concubinage were normal. The Chosen People

[1] Sheed and Ward, New York, 1967.

had to grow out of the worship of strange gods—the worship often enough being stranger than the gods. Solomon, who built the great Temple to the true God, built altars also to the gods of his countless wives. Since the enslavement or massacre of their defeated enemies seemed to those far-off people, in their beginnings and for long after, wholly right, they assumed that God wanted these things. Therefore they said He did.

Slowly they grew away from much of this. But they also had to grow in the knowledge of God, and of the meaning and destiny of man. After their return from Captivity in Babylon we find them wholly monotheist, as no people had ever been. But God had not revealed his own innermost life to them in the doctrine of the Trinity. Sanctifying Grace, the key to St. Paul's mind and indeed to everything that the Church does and teaches, is not explicitly stated anywhere in the Old Testament. Nor is Redemption as Christ revealed it—although it runs all through the Old Testament, but applied almost entirely to a worldly exaltation of the Chosen People. Of life after death there are traces early, but of the Resurrection of the Body only at the end, and of the Beatific Vision not at all. God's love is there and the love we should have for God; love of neighbor is less evident; but for love of enemies we must await Christ.

Yet for those who know its ultimate fulfillment in Christ, reading the Old Testament—seeing men moving toward this fulfillment—is a rich experience. And there is something else. With all that they lacked, the Chosen People had a living awareness of God's majesty and holiness, a living conviction of

God's personality and nearness, which can make the reading of the Old Testament an electrifying experience for us.

3

The New Testament is nineteen hundred years old. For a large part of that time the mass of Catholics have respected and neglected it. Suddenly there is a new emphasis, the beginning of a new excitement. It looks—almost—as if the New Testament might become a living element in the life of the plain Catholic, like Sunday Mass or devotion to our Lady. What difference will it make if it does?

Today, we run into a problem that was not there twenty years ago—the effect of Form Criticism upon Catholic scholars, or more precisely, the effect of one school of Form Criticism, Rudolf Bultmann's, upon the second rank of Catholic scholars. Somewhere between the great scholars and ourselves come the middlemen. Great Catholic scholars would blush, if they could hear what the popularizers—in forums and college classrooms—make of their own carefully thought, carefully stated, findings.

As the New Learning reached the rank and file what it seemed to be saying was that the Gospels give us no certain information about Christ: what they give is the early Church's "reconstruction."

Bultmann had the new Christians invent things done and things said by Christ to justify what was in fact being done and taught by the Church. Catholics accepted the invention, but upon a higher motive—the incidents and speeches attributed to

Christ expressed the Church's inward experience of Him. In either event, the factuality was not what mattered but the meaning: and the meaning was the same whether or not the things actually happened!

In these last few years there has been a change. The "ranking" Protestant scholar is no longer Bultmann but, perhaps, Oscar Cullmann who thinks that most of the things did happen. But meanwhile large numbers of Catholic college students had lost their faith in a Christ presented to them as if He were no more than a figure in one of His own Parables.

He had already become just that to too many Catholics without the aid of the Form Critics. Ignorance of the Scriptures, said St. Jerome, is ignorance of Christ: St. Jerome would have been horrified at our generation's ignorance. There is a lack of the background without which our Lord's words and acts lose so much of their significance—what Pharisees and Sadducees were, what Rome was doing in Palestine, who the Herod was who had the infants massacred in Bethlehem, and the Herod who had the Baptist beheaded, and the Herod who caused the first Apostle to be martyred.

What matters more is the lack of elementary knowledge about our Lord Himself as the Gospels show Him—whatever one's view of their factuality. Even if nothing matters but their "meaning," the portrait they give us of Christ is that meaning's essence. The Gospel Christ is not at present part of the plain Catholic's equipment (see p. 174). He knows about the birth, Passion and Death; but of His public life, only bits and pieces. The Rosary is partly to blame, jumping straight from the Finding in the Temple to the Agony in the Garden. (Why isn't there another set of Mysteries between the Joyful and the Sorrowful? What incidents would be included, I wonder, and what would the Five be called?)

As to what the Acts and the Epistles tell us of Him there are not even bits and pieces. In all the New Testament we are told of only one virtue that Christ our Lord learned. We have had the text already, as surprising as any in the whole of Scripture. Listen to it again: "Although he was a Son, he learned *obedience* through what he suffered; and being made perfect, he became the source of eternal salvation to all who *obey* him" (Heb 5:8–9 [RSV]).

Imagine all the sermons that could be preached on that! To imagine, indeed, is all that most of us are in a position to do, for we haven't heard even one. In fact I think it is rare for our preachers to draw on any part of Scripture not in the Sunday Gospels. Evidently they feel that, given our want of general knowledge, these are all they can safely quote from. But if congregations ever become gospel-soaked, epistle-soaked, what sermons could be preached to them!

But of course what matters most in New Testament reading is the intimacy with our Lord, which is not to be obtained without it. When Catholics drop religion they are refusing Christ. A Christ barely known is only too easy to refuse. They feel they have "seen through" the Faith, when they have never really seeen Christ at all.

Into my head there floats a ridiculous episode of thirty years back. I was at a Catholic Evidence Guild meeting in Franklin Park, Washington. A questioner announced that he had been brought up a Catholic, but had become a Protestant as a result of reading the New Testament. The speaker said "Did you marry her?" "Yes," said the questioner "How did you know?"

As I say, a ridiculous episode. I quote it only because of the two points of view which meet here head-on—the old-fashioned Protestant assumption that Catholics only remain so because the Church keeps them from reading the Bible; and the speaker's assumption that the Bible contains nothing to shake a Catholic's faith in the Church. Both assumptions will be tested if Gospels and Epistles really do enter the Catholic bloodstream.

At one level—the highest—they have been tested already. No scripture scholar, whatever his religion, doubts that his Catholic co-workers love both Church and Bible: no group of experts but would be glad to have, say, the Dominican Père Benoit working with them, as the Harvard Divinity School had Père de Vaux. But what will happen down where the rest of men live?

Both for discussion with Protestants, and to get the most profit out of it for himself, the plain Catholic will need to see just what Scripture is. Neither Testament is a manual of theology. Both treat of God's dealings with men and men's responses, but not as treatises. From end to end of the Bible's million words, there is no ordered statement of any single area of revelation—no drawing together into essay form of what we are to know about God, or human life, or sin, or redemption, or what follows death, nothing remotely approaching a treatise on the Church.

About the Gospels, remember two things: (1)

The writers are not telling us all they know of Christ. Out of the illimitable richness of Christ and His meaning for men, each made his selection according to his purpose in writing: at the end of John we get an admission of the incompleteness and a statement of the purpose. "Now Jesus did many other signs . . . which are not written in this book; but these are written that you may believe that Jesus is the Christ, the Son of God, and that believing you may have life in his name" (20:30–1 [RSV]). (2) The Gospels were written for people who had already received a basic instruction in the truths of the religion they were accepting. If this interests you, read Luke 1:1–4, Gal 1:9; 2:2, 9; 1 Cor 11:23; 15:3; 2 Tim 1:13; 2 Thess 2:14.

But of that basic instruction we have no written record; one who accepts the Gospels but not a teaching Church is forced to treat them as sufficient in themselves, which they are not. The Evangelists are concerned with developing and enriching the understanding of *what their readers already know.*

So is St. Paul. He writes of elements in the doctrines which have been misunderstood or even denied; of elements on which he has new light to shed; of new problems to which doctrines must be applied. But there is no "syllabus," so to speak, no synthesis. He assumes this as already known. So do John and Peter and James and Jude, and whoever wrote Hebrews. They take the Church, for instance, absolutely for granted. Paul calls it "the household of God, which is the church of the living God, the pillar and the ground of truth" (1 Tim 3:15). But he does not describe its structure, or the area of its authority, or the way it functions.

When Christ left the world He had already committed to the Apostles a body of truth for the instruction of the human race, and promised to be with them in their teaching till the end of time. They taught it, they trained others to teach it, and the Church has taught it from that day to this. But it is nowhere set out in Scripture. There is no reason why any given element of it should have been written down in the New Testament, unless someone was being wrong about it, or some problem had arisen which involved it, or the writer had caught fire from it.

So the absence from the New Testament of some teaching or practice of the Church does not prove anything either way. There would be difficulty only if in some matter the one contradicted the other. But in forty-seven years of meeting all and sundry in outdoor meetings and indoor conferences, I have never found any such contradiction—though problem passages in plenty. And in the three or four hundred years since the Reformation settled down, we do not find many who have left the Church on Scriptural grounds. Which is why the speaker in Franklin Park was so certain that his questioner hadn't.

In the Teaching Church and Scripture we have two ways of approach, God-aided, to one same revelation—two different ways, each bringing its own light. Each supplements the other, very much as the medical textbook is supplemented by studies of individual cases. Books written to meet actual situations naturally seem more vital than formal, orderly statements of the reality to be taught; but for teaching and for guidance, in medicine or religion, these last are essential.

I have said that I personally have never found

any contradiction. But I see why non-Catholics do. And that brings us to the heart of ecumenical dialogue.

3

I wonder how many outdoor hecklers have asked me "Why do you believe the Bible, anyway?" It's always been a key question between Christians and unbelievers. But the surge of Ecumenism has made it a key question among Christians. Catholics and Protestants and Jews and unbelievers work together in all fraternity on the text of Scripture, studying ancient manuscripts of both Testaments, discovering similarities in the documents of the pagan religions, reading one another avidly. But what's it all about? What is the value of Scripture in its totality, what authority has it, how far are you and I bound by it? The answers we give depend on why we accept it. I have never been at an ecumenical gathering of the top men—leaders of Churches, world-ranking theologians and Scripture scholars. But I'd love to be a fly on the ceiling when they came to these questions.

That men of all Christian faiths agree in accepting the Bible is wonderful. But what do they think it *is?* What do they accept it *as?* Does their common acceptance in fact mean agreement? Nothing divides men more than disagreement about something both accept. Two Christians can reach a point of bitterness about the Bible which neither could reach in discussing it with a Mohammedan. I long ago discovered that it's easy to feel brotherly with my Mohammedan hecklers!

To my street-corner questioners I had my answer

ready: I accept the Bible because the Church which Christ commissioned to teach men till the end of time gives it to me as God's inspired word. The Bible makes no such claim for itself. But men who do not accept the Church do acccept the Bible. Why? That question will have to be faced if Ecumenism is to progress; indeed if the Bible is to do the fullness of its work in men's souls. A gentlemen's agreement not to discuss it—"after all we do accept the Bible; why start an argument?"—will not do. The Bible's authority is bound up with our reason for accepting it.

When the Dogma of our Lady's Assumption into heaven was defined in 1950 the Anglican Archbishops of Canterbury and York issued a moving protest, not against the doctrine's truth but against the Church's right to define it. Their Church, they said, "refuses to regard as requisite for saving faith any doctrine or opinions not plainly contained in the Scriptures".

I wish they had had to defend that against my outdoor hecklers—indeed, I wish everybody who has any religious statement to make would make a point of trying it out first on the man in the street. On the words "plainly contained in the Scriptures," the Archbishops would have had trouble with one heckler in particular, a man learned in Scripture who has troubled me often enough. There is not a key text on which he, and his scholarly fellows, cannot advance a variety of interpretations. It goes with the nature of language that it is practically impossible to write a sentence for which only one meaning is possible—that is why lawyers grow rich.

That objection applies to any document. But

there is another which applies particularly to the New Testament. As we have noted, to treat the New Testament as all-inclusive—so that what it does not contain is excluded—is to treat it as it was not written. The writers were writing for people who had already received a basic instruction on entering the Church, an instruction carried on by Apostles and men appointed or approved by them. The writers were not giving this all over again; they assumed it was known and went on to clarify or apply or emphasize particular elements in it. The New Testament was never meant to stand alone: it was written to be read within the framework of Church teaching. Ecumenical discussions must take account of this simple fact. As a fly on the ceiling I would listen with growing excitement.

At any rate, the old Church-versus-Bible line-up hardly exists now. On the Catholic side, we have Pope Pius XII saying that without Biblical theology dogmatic theology is sterile, and Vatican II saying that "the study of the sacred writings is, as it were, the soul of sacred theology" (*Revelation* 24). On the Protestant side there is a growing realization of the Church, and of a continuous stream of teaching (what Catholics call "tradition") —a realization highly developed in some, embryonic in others, but nowhere wholly absent.

More and more, I think, the feeling grows that a living Church, with authority to apply God's revelation to situations as they happen and to questions only now being asked, would have a certain advantage over Scripture which is still, and will remain forever, as it was written.

With authority, I say. All ecumenical dialogue

must come to that if it is to move from an exchange of courtesies to a sharing of minds. The Bible has authority, but just what? And based upon what? Has the Church authority?

4

If I were not already a Catholic, would I find the Church in the New Testament? I *might* not, obviously. Millions who know their Bibles extraordinarily well don't. But might I? In other words is the Church actually *there*? And if it is, why doesn't everybody see it?

To repeat, the New Testament was written for people who were members of the Church, receiving its sacraments, above all receiving its doctrinal and moral teaching—obeying it, disobeying it, understanding it, misunderstanding it. The Acts of the Apostles tells of happenings within the Church, especially its breaking out into the Gentile world, thirty years in thirty chapters; the Epistles—a dozen or so covering some fifteen years—are a kind of running commentary on the disobedience and the misunderstandings, along with wonderful flashes of light and fire from the hearts of the writers. But its writers assume the nature and structure of the Church as known.

From what does get written—in this unorganized, unplanned way—I and millions of Catholics feel that the Church which is being written about is the Church we know: in the praise or in the blame, we feel wholly at home. There is simply nothing to shake our absolute assumption that this is the Church we know.

Take the two "binding and loosing" texts (Mt 16:19 and 18:18): "whatsoever" Peter, or the Apostles as a group, should decide to forbid or permit, Heaven would ratify the decision. The Church of the New Testament took that quite literally; so does ours today. What other does? "Let him be anathema," said St. Paul (Gal 1:9): and "a man that is a heretic, after a first and second admonition, avoid" (Tit 3:10). Our Church may have used "anathema" too freely, "heretic" too loosely—but the phrases belong to the language we've heard all our lives.

The Protestant reader knows all this as well as we do. Nor does he hold that the present division of Christendom into scores, or hundreds, of Churches all differing in their teaching belongs in the New Testament or would have been thought tolerable by the Apostles. Well, then, why doesn't he become a Catholic? He will probably answer that we will find the Church of the first Christians neither in the Catholic Church nor in the Protestant churches and that that is what we must work to restore.

And there is indeed one stain upon us and upon them—all the Christian churches that have had the power have at some time "persecuted." When the Pope meets the Archbishop of Canterbury I doubt if they talk about Cranmer, whom we burnt at the stake, or about the Anabaptist Joan Bocher, whom Cranmer burnt at the stake.

But deviations from the ideal do not settle the question. After all, no crime, no blindness with which Christians can be charged exceeds the criminality and blindness of the People of God, God's Chosen People, as the Old Testament presents them. Scandals will come, Christ warned His followers. Awareness of this simple, complex truth must be strong in us as we look again at our question: Are Catholics deceiving themselves in feeling so wholly at home in the Church of the New Testament? Is it actually there?

Come back to a text of Hebrews 5 which these days is never out of my mind—I have already quoted it twice in these pages—"Although Christ was Son, he learned obedience through what he suffered; and being made perfect he became the source of eternal salvation to all who obey him." Obedience at one end—whether His to His Father, or ours to Him—implies authority at the other: and an authority made known to us. How are we to obey Christ if we do not know what His commands are?

Even if the New Testament contained all the details of His "whatsoever I have commanded you" —which it does not and could not—the *words* would not be enough, given the vast variety of the meanings men have somehow managed to draw from those we have got. If we had only the words, we should be reduced to following our own best opinion of what He would have wanted and that is not what obedience means.

"He that hears you hears me"—He said that to the disciples He was sending out (Luke 10:16). *Men, authorized by Him and guaranteed by Him against error*—that is *His* formula. It is the formula in operation throughout the New Testament. Insofar as there have been deformations of it, additions that do not go with it, the whole purpose of the Second Vatican Council was to cleanse and restore.

To that formula Protestants and Catholics alike must be conformed. It sounds *very* Catholic to me: but for us too it will mean reappraisals, and some of them may to some of us be agonizing.

5
Mass and Eucharist

For the man-in-the-pew the question, "Is it the same Church?" often enough boils down to the question, "Is it the same Mass?" The changes there are so obvious—the high altar practically ignored and the tabernacle hard to find; the priest facing the people when he isn't sitting with folded hands, while members of the congregation read aloud; fasting before Communion reduced almost out of existence; Latin yielding place to English, all expected to dialogue, and to sing as they go to Communion; no last Gospel; octaves banished from Epiphany, Ascension, Corpus Christi. If he reads the papers he finds startling things said and startling things suggested—about the Real Presence, our Lady's virginity, what you will. There is hardly a doctrine or practice of the Church one has not heard attacked by a priest. He finds it all very confusing, rather disturbing, but not very real, in the nature of the stage direction "Noises off."

But the Mass is close to him. If only they would leave the Mass alone, he feels, he could go on practicing his Faith till it all blows over. He had loved the Mass; he knew where he was in it. And now they have changed it without a word of consultation with him or his sort. He wouldn't have made a grievance of that, for the Church has no habit of consulting the laity, if they hadn't just been telling him of the laity's priesthood—and the Mass is the priestliest action of all.

For myself, I found it hard to get used to the new way. It was after some weeks of the changed ritual that I answered the priest's words "The Body of Christ" with "Thank you" (but then ritual isn't my strong point—I once poured wine instead of water over the priest's fingers at the Lavabo). But I like most of the changes (I don't like the hymn-singing, especially when I am at the altar rail; I am not given to singing at meals). But there are still many who dislike the "new" Mass bitterly.

It is partly a matter of emotional attachment to something one has always had. Changing it feels like an uprooting. There was a time in the Eastern Church when men were slaying one another over the question whether the priest's blessing should be given with one finger upraised or two. I have met people really uneasy at the Pope's abolition of the Lenten fast—one remembers the reaction of the Irish in the last century when Pope Leo XIII, who had just condemned an effort by the tenants to win justice from the landlords, dispensed them from abstinence because of an influenza epidemic. Better for him, they said, if he left politics alone and minded his religion.

Things we have grown used to come to seem of

the essence. It does us good to re-examine them, and learn what is or is not essential. We are hearing it said that, in this matter of changes in the Mass, the Church is admitting that Luther was right after all. But—as Luther knew—the use of the vernacular instead of Latin is a detail compared with the doctrine of the Mass as a Sacrifice; receiving the Eucharist in both kinds is a trifle compared with whether, or in what sense, Christ our Lord is really present in either kind; just as whether priests may marry is a trifle compared with the reality of the Apostolic Succession.

It is pretty certain that we are not at the end of changes. Catholics with their eyes fixed on the Last Supper want to be rid of vestments and see Mass restored to the dining room: my wife remembers back fifteen years to the first time she was at a Mass said by a priest-workman at the kitchen table, and very moving she found it. But it was a long way from the ideal of those to whom Mass means Latin murmured in a dark Church. And there are those to whom Church music means Gregorian Chant in a Gothic Abbey (like the buzzing of bees in a bottle, an irreverent friend of mine said): they may not be enthusiastic about the Missa Luba of African Catholics or the Flamenco-style Mass now being prepared in Spain.

I have mentioned the priest—at a Church for which I have a special love—who was so seized with the doctrine of the priesthood of the laity that he would put the Host into the hands of communicants so that they might minister it to themselves. That practice was stopped. But it may return—who knows? After all it happened that way in the earlier centuries.

Who knows indeed? The question "what next?" sets the tone of all present discussion of the Mass. Changes which have happened, changes which may happen, are argued over passionately wherever Catholics meet. The quietest people find themselves shouting. We are back in the fourth century when men would have the cutting of their hair interrupted while the barber argued about the relation of Father and Son in the Trinity.

We are right to see the Liturgy as vitally important. It was no accident that the recent Vatican Council gave itself first to Liturgical Revival and Development. *The Mass is the one place where we meet God, not as individuals (which we can do at any moment) but as His People.* Unless this meeting is right, nothing else in the Church will be.

The Council thought that the Mass matters. So do we of the laity. But we and the Council may not always have been on the same wavelength. When Pope Paul spoke, as he did at a weekly audience, of a devout layman who "was happy because *for the first time in his life* he had participated in the Sacrifice of the Mass to the full spiritual measure", many of us were forced to rethink the Mass. What is this "full spiritual measure" which is made possible by the changes in the ritual? Have we all these years been content with some lesser measure?

The key is perhaps contained in the phrase in which discontent at the changes is often expressed —"There's no peace." Those to whom Mass was a time for being alone with God feel that the congregation is crowding in on the intimacy of their converse with Him. And in the din of the dialogue they can't hear themselves pray.

In all this there is a profound spirituality, but it may be missing the point of the Mass. "Liturgical services are not private functions," says the Council. We go to Mass *in order to* join with others in an action we and they are performing together. And that action-with-others is not simply praying, as when we say the Rosary together or sing the *Te Deum*. It is the offering to God of Christ once slain on Calvary and now forever living, as Vatican II expressed it (*The Church* 28)—"until the coming of the Lord, the one sacrifice of the New Testament —the sacrifice of Christ offering himself once and for all to His Father as a spotless victim—is represented and applied in the Sacrifice of the Mass" (cf. Heb 9:11–28).

The priest consecrates and offers in the power of Christ; and we are not merely spectators watching or an audience listening, however devotionally. We are partners in the offering: *"my sacrifice and yours,"* says the priest to us at the *Orate fratres*. The Council gives our priesthood rich expression. "The faithful join in the offering of the Eucharist by virtue of their royal priesthood" (*The Church* 10). "The faithful offer the Immaculate Victim not only through the hands of the priest but also *with him"* (*Liturgy* 48).

Compared with the immensity of what is being done at Mass, questions of Latin or vernacular, silence or dialogue, are secondary—not unimportant but not primary either. We cannot profitably argue about how the Mass should be said till we have brought our whole mind to bear upon what the Mass is.

What in hard fact is our state of mind, our state of spirit, during Mass? In his poem *Christmas*

Eve and Easter Day Robert Browning describes Catholics at Mass:

> All famishing with expectation
> Of the main altar's consummation.

Happy you and I if that is our state. But is it? Let us admit that we don't all, or always, look as if we were famishing, or even particularly expectant.

Not that that proves anything. The Host does not look as if Christ were present in it, the communicant often enough does not look as if Christ were present in him. In neither instance does the look tell the whole story. But at least we know that it is hard to maintain realization at full intensity. We have had the experience of the Mass so often that we hardly experience it any more.

Considering the immensity of what Christ is doing, one would think it impossible for the mind to wander for so much as an instant. An instant? Distraction can occupy half our Mass time. I haven't a doubt that men have died for the Mass who suffered distraction at every Mass they ever heard.

Even those who feel nostalgia for the Mass that is gone can hardly deny that they feel less distraction from what is being done at the altar at the new dialogued Mass in the vernacular. As Pope Paul put it at one of his weekly audiences: "Previously our presence was sufficient; now attention is demanded, and action. Previously one could doze, but no longer."

To be free from distraction because there is constantly something for us to say is at least better than day-dreaming. And the words we now find ourselves saying, and saying aloud, with men on each side of us saying them too, can do strange things to us. But ideally we should be held by what the Mass exists to do: that should become so real to us, so in-built, that *of itself* it grips our whole mind and heart.

We should be livingly conscious of what Mass is, conscious not only of what is being done but of ourselves as taking part in the doing. The Church, says the Council in a stunning phrase, is the sacrament of the salvation of the whole world: and the Mass is a sort of burning-glass focusing that sacrament.

Or rather it focuses Christ. Ask the first dozen Christians you meet—"What is Christ doing now?" Unless one can answer that, one cannot understand the Mass. Over the years I have put the question to crowds in Hyde Park, London, and Times Square, New York. Those who don't care naturally have no answer. But even many who truly love our Lord cannot imagine anything He need do now— after all, He said on the Cross, "It is finished."

It is rare to have anyone quote, "He is living on *to make intercession for us*," still less the words which precede these—"Jesus continues for ever and *his priestly office is unchanging:* that is why He can give eternal salvation to those who through Him make their way to God" (Heb 7:24–25). "Christ has entered into heaven itself, now to appear in the presence of God on our behalf" (Heb 9:24 [RSV]).

So that is what He is doing now and always— making intercession for us as priest. How? By "standing as a lamb slain" (Apoc 5). He appears before God with the marks of His wounding showing, glowing.

His redeeming sacrifice—Death, Resurrection, Ascension—was complete, but it still has to be applied to each individual human being, and it is by this that he applies it.

That is Christ's work "on our behalf" in heaven. Because He wills it so, it breaks through to our altars. The priest in His name, by His power, offers the same Christ—there on the altar in the appearance of bread and wine—to the same Father for the same saving purpose. Christ is doing this at the altar, the priest is doing it with Him. And we are doing it too.

How do we of the laity come in? In St. Thomas' phrase, Baptism is a sharing in the priesthood of Christ, and so is Confirmation; with Holy Orders priesthood here on earth is completed, but even without that we have some part in Christ the Priest. By Baptism we are elements in the Body of that Christ who is being offered, in whose power the priest makes the offering, and we with him. We cannot help being part of the action of the Mass. We can only behave as if we were not.

It is strange that we should ever forget this prime fact about our baptized selves. We are nobody in particular but, compared with members of Christ, no one is anybody! It is strangest of all if we forget it at Mass—if we "go to" Mass not seeing our Lord as He is in heaven, offering Himself, once slain but now forever living, to His Father; not seeing the priest and ourselves, in the power of what is happening in heaven, offering the same Lord to the same Father. If we do thus *see* Mass, we are in a better position to discuss the changes.

2

When, with the Council in full flow, Pope Paul issued an encyclical on the Blessed Eucharist the ordinary Catholic was puzzled. The Council was deeply involved with quite different questions: what was so urgent about this one? The document itself did nothing to relieve his puzzlement. It was simply the straight doctrine of the Eucharist as he had know it all his Catholic life.

But that was precisely why the Pope issued it. In various parts of the Church theologians were uttering—not to one another but to the public— views which questioned, or rather denied, almost every element in the doctrine as Catholics had always known it. The Pope must speak or the Eucharist was in peril.

There were theories of Christ's presence in the sacrament which at least sounded like a denial of its reality—the word "real" was preserved but not in any sense of the word "reality" common among men. And the view was spreading that, in whatever sense Christ was present in the sacrament, He was there only to be received as food: so that any other use of the consecrated Host was a superstitious abuse.

Thus in many places visits to the Blessed Sacrament were discouraged—even mocked: the Tabernacle was made almost impossible to find; Benediction was dropped. There were those who added a kind of postscript to all this with an insistence that the Host belonged so totally to one Mass only, that in some places people (seminarians among them) were refusing to receive hosts consecrated at an earlier Mass.

It was in this situation, not universal but existent and spreading, and with more than a beginning of chaos in it, that Pope Paul issued *Mysterium Fidei*.

No Catholic theologian, I have said, denied Christ's presence in the Eucharist: but it is profoundly mysterious, nothing in human experience is in the least like it; the inquiring mind is constantly drawn by it, in a sense tantalized by it, driven to seek for ways of "explaining" it.

Transubstantiation was one such effort, magnificent, rich in itself, rich in suggestion of further depths. But it did not answer every question. Some minds found more satisfaction in it than others. It preserved the essence of the truth Christ had committed to the Church through the Apostles, but it was born of a philosophy not congenial to many of today's thinkers. They felt that there might be another approach to the explication of the mystery.

In *Mysterium Fidei* the Pope does nothing to discourage this. But he insists that the essence of the mystery is inviolate, and he names certain modern theories—transfiguration, trans-signification and others—as not in harmony with it.

What is the essence? Christ had said "This is my body." The Pope reiterates that the consecrated Host *is* His body, that what the chalice contains *is* His blood. The one looks like bread, the other like wine; they react to every test as bread reacts and wine reacts. But they are not bread, not wine: they cannot be since they are His body, His blood. The Pope quotes St. Cyril of Jerusalem: "That which seems to be bread is not bread, though it tastes like it, but the Body of Christ."

"It is presence in the fullest sense," the Pope reminds us, "that is, it is a substantial presence by which Christ, the God-man, is wholly and entirely present." Symbolism will not do as an explanation: after consecration "a new reality is present which may justly be termed ontological, something quite different from what was there before."

This difference, what we may call the "real absence" of bread, is shown as the test. "Presence" is a wide term; there are so many ways of being present. But there is one plain way of being absent, namely, not being there. Any solution, the Pope makes clear, must accept the fact that bread and wine are no longer there. The absence of bread is not the most important fact about the Blessed Eucharist, but it is the most instant test of any theory about it.

After the consecration Christ is really, substantially, present: there are the appearances of bread but no bread, of wine but no wine. We are receiving Christ Himself within our own being—that is what matters. *How* this can be we do not know, but for the fact of it we have Christ's word. In comparison with the *fact*, the *how* is of no importance. Yet men long to see deeper, to find explanations—what happens to our Lord's height, for instance, and to His weight? What causes our palates to taste bread as we receive the Host?

Transubstantiation leaves so much still dark. And the Encyclical looks for further exploration of the mystery to arrive at "greater clarity, greater accuracy." But it imposes two conditions: (1) the Reality of Christ's presence must not be dimmed or diminished; (2) no individual may "on his own authority modify the formulas used by the Council of Trent." A theologian may propose modifications or even different theories, discuss them with other theologians, offer them to the Church: but he may not teach them as Catholic doctrine till the Church has approved them. "Unless you shall eat the flesh of the Son of Man and drink His blood you shall not have life in you," says our Lord. With eternal life thus involved, the Eucharist is too important for the faithful to have the speculation of any individual, however richly gifted, imposed upon them.

Obviously every man must read Scripture for himself. But to me it seems that Paul the Saint and Paul the Pope are entirely in accord. "The cup that we bless, is it not the blood of the Lord? The bread that we break, is it not the body of the Lord?" That is in 1 Corinthians 10. In the following chapter come two texts: "He who eats the bread and drinks the cup unworthily will be guilty of profaning the body and blood of the Lord"; "He who eats and drinks without discerning the Lord's body and blood eats and drinks damnation to himself." These would be incredible things to say of any mere symbol, of anything less indeed than what Pope Paul calls "the presence by which Christ the God-man is wholly and entirely present."

But what of the Tabernacle? And visits? And Benediction? What, that is, of the view given wide utterance by theologians but rejected by *Mysterium Fidei,* that the Eucharist was given us by our Lord to be used only as food, given for nourishment *not* for adoration? As with so many other problems of either-or, the answer is both. Our Lord did indeed consecrate bread so that it was changed into His body to be received as food, wine so that it was changed into His Blood to be received as drink. But He did not say "only," and common sense not only does not require "only" but actually excludes it.

It would seem unnatural to the last degree to concentrate on the nourishing power of the food while ignoring what the food actually is. Christ our Lord does not come upon our altars in order to be adored but to nourish. But He who thus comes *is* adorable and it would be highly artificial to act as though we did not know this. Our Lord in the Host does not become less nourishing by being adored, and the act of adoration has its own way of nourishing the human spirit.

There are those who would abolish the Elevation at Mass on the ground that it was introduced only because at the time the faithful did not frequently receive the Eucharist. Maybe so. But how splendidly the Elevation has justified itself, securing its place in the Mass on its own merits. Who would wish to forgo this moment in which we join together in adoring Him whom we are individually to receive?

Christ's body is still present in the Host after Mass, says the Encyclical. Therefore, although ideally it is best to receive a host at the Mass of its Consecration, Hosts consecrated at one Mass may be received at another and may be received also by the sick wherever they may be. These Hosts are normally kept in a Tabernacle in the Church. The practice grew of visiting the Church and praying before the Tabernacle in full consciousness of the Presence within it. Legalistic types extend their objection against the Elevation even more violently to this practice: they want the

Tabernacle to be kept out of sight so that people might not be tempted to adore Him who is most certainly there. On the same principle they are against Benediction of the Blessed Sacrament.

Life is larger than logic, especially that kind of logic. The experience of praying before the Tabernacle is its own justification. We rejoiced in the learned defence of it by the Jesuit Karl Rahner. And the Encyclical is wholly for our comfort. "Christ wishes to ensure His presence among us without limits of time"—and His presence calls us to adore. "The faithful should be encouraged to return love for love in visiting the Blessed Sacrament."

You know the jingle:

> Whenever I am near a Church
> I go to pay a visit
> So that when I'm carried in
> Our Lord won't say "Who is it?"

A theologian might blench at that, but as a mere human man he might sometimes find himself repeating it all the same, when no theologians were around—they make one another self-conscious.

3

In all sorts of ways, we feel, Mass is not what it used to be. Let us glance at some of our present discontents.

The discontents are not the same for everybody. I have mine, you have yours. But there are two main groups of us: those who feel that the changes don't go far enough; and those who loved the Mass as it was.

For the moment we concentrate upon these. They vary from people, like me, who are unhappy about individual changes, and people to whom any change seems like a rending of some part of their being, a treason against the sacrifice of the Mass itself. It would be wrong to write this off as emotional, irrational. Rationality cannot say everything in religion, any more than in the rest of life; and there are sacred emotions as well as profane or merely neutral.

But, for those who feel like this about the changes, it may be steadying to be reminded that our Roman Mass is the result of a long development. At the last Supper, our Lord "faced the people" and spoke in Aramaic. If a time-machine could have brought Peter from the first century into ours, he would not easily have followed High Mass in St. Peter's—the Latin particularly would have bothered him; he had come to Rome late in life.

Latin is not an eighth sacrament; but those who see something special in it are surely right. It was a newcomer on the Christian scene, but for us of the West it has been prayed in and thought in and taught in as no other language has. There would be an insensitiveness in merely dropping it like a bad habit we have outgrown, and the champions of Mass in Latin have quite an argument in some of the English we are hearing. The translations seem to have been made by scholars who cannot clean from their own pens the Latinity in which they have so long been dipped: much of the phrasing sounds like Latin's vengeance on its supplanter.

The most spectacular oddity is, of course, "Go, the Mass is ended." "Thanks be to God," we reply piously to this incredible statement about a sacrifice which will not "end" while the world endures. Hell must have burst into applause the first time that phrase was heard from the altar. But it is not the only strangeness we hear. I hope it is not disrespectful of me to find myself so often remembering what was once said about something quite different —"The man who wrote that may have ears, for so has another animal. He certainly hasn't an ear."

But we should remember both that our own Church Latin would have sounded monstrous to Cicero, and that the new versions are rush jobs and will be improved. Our real discontents go deeper. I give two of my own, not because I am necessarily right about them but because they enable us to get at what should be the governing principles of change.

I dislike the playing down of the Offertory prayers: the prayer *Deus qui humanae substantiae* contains the sole reminder in the Ordinary of the Mass that we are to be partakers of Christ's divinity: I cannot imagine any hymn valuable enough to drown out that.

I dislike the proposed merging into one, or dropping altogether, of the two Confiteors at the beginning of the Mass. The dropping obviously, but the merging just as certainly, would destroy a dramatic interchange which is a key to the cooperation in worship of priests and lay people. The priest confesses that he has sinned exceedingly, and we pray Almighty God to have mercy on him: then we confess that we are just as bad, and the priest prays Almighty God to have mercy on us. Each party has uttered its own unworthiness and accepted the utterance of the other's. The Mass can begin.

I may be wrong about either or both of my "dislikes". But a principle is involved. There are those who set up a pattern and by it Liturgy must be measured. It may be what was done in the early Church; or what has been done for centuries; or some Platonic ideal of what a Liturgy ought to be. In none of these patterns are our present human values—our needs, our feelings—allowed for. And without human values Liturgy grows corpse-like. What our Lord said of the Sabbath can be applied here—the Liturgy was made for man, not man for the Liturgy.

Our approach to God *together with others* calls for an accepted order not needed by our private and individual prayers—we cannot all be acting together separately, so to speak. This accepted order is Liturgy. A liturgy must please God, or it is pointless; but also it must express the mind and heart of the worshippers, or it is lifeless. To keep alive, a liturgy may have to change.

Rituals which were wholly right for yesterday's man may be empty forms for today's. Rituals developed in one country may be meaningless in another—where we of the West bend the knee, for instance, the Japanese bow; the kissing of the Missal at the Gospel says nothing at all to the Japanese, who are not a kissing people. And within the one country and the one age, there are differences from one man to the next—to one a sanctuary lamp glowing in a dark church is that and no more, to another it can be a reminder that he is not alone in a dark world too powerful for him.

Two principles emerge. The first is that the liturgy must be formed—and necessary changes in it must be made—not by individuals according to their taste and fancy; not by each pastor for his own congregation, still less by each curate (I have mentioned elsewhere the curate whose dislike of the Rosary exploded into hysteria one day in the pulpit). The Vatican Council has laid it down, in the Constitution, on the Liturgy, that even a priest may not "add, remove or change anything in the liturgy on his own authority."

The second is that the liturgy will not accomplish its purpose unless it expresses the mind and heart, the consciousness and even the unconsciousness, of the worshippers. At a given time the authorities might lose contact with the people; but the liturgical expert can be out of contact even more completely.

It is strange, come to think of it, how much time and passion we give to the changes—Latin, dialogue and the like—and how little of either we give to the Mass itself. Yet unless that is alive in us the changes can only galvanize, giving a show of life but no new vitality. A change in the congregation will do more than any number of changes in the liturgy.

The essence of that profounder change is in the living awareness of what is being done at the altar, and of our active part in it. I have had the chance to hear Catholics questioned on the first point: some thought that our Lord is slain at every Mass; some thought the Mass a meal only with Christ present symbolically; and between these extremes there was devotion but not much clarity.

Remember what Browning says of Mass (in *Easter Eve and Christmas Day*):

> Earth breaks up, time drops away,
> In flows heaven, with its new day
> Of endless life.

That is not to be dismissed as poetry; the phrase "In flows heaven" is precise. Look again at what the two texts we have just discussed (Hebrews 7:24–5, 9:24 and Apocalypse 5) tell us of the Mass. In Heaven Christ stands always before His Father, presenting Himself once slain upon Calvary and forever living, "interceding" for the salvation of men. At the altar the priest, by Christ's command, in Christ's power, offers that same Christ, present as really, to the same Father for the same purpose. And we take part with the priest in the offering— we and the priest are lifted into one action with the Redeeming Christ.

Did Browning know that? An interesting question. But there is a question that matters more to you and me: Do *we* know it? Upon that we can test ourselves. At Mass are we conscious of Christ in heaven "standing as a Lamb slain," "living on to make intercession for us"? Do we remind ourselves of the relation to *that* of what is about to take place at the altar? And of our own part in it, and the part of every other person at Mass with us, and of our consequent oneness with them? Do we even know the three texts? If that is how we do see the Mass, we must see ritual changes as secondary. Latin or Greek or Hottentot, Swahili or Calithumpian, vestments or day-clothes, dialogue or silence, basilica or somebody's house or open sky, altar or kitchen table—how can we spare a thought to these, considering what is actually being done by Christ, by the priest, by ourselves?

Yet the rituals matter. We are not pure spirits, not sheer minds. There is a harmony possible between the spiritual and the material, and liturgy must serve it. We do not join in the offering of the Mass with minds free from care, problems, temptation. Material things—words, gestures, postures— can concentrate us, or leave us unaffected, or add a further distraction of their own. I have seen a quotation from the new Spanish Missal—a man needs "a spiritual counterweight to the whirl of his life." Our Mass *should* be that. May the changes, already made or on the way, help it to be.

Our private prayer is the approach to God of the individual self which each of us uniquely is, and it changes as we change. Liturgy is the corporate approach of men to God (the angels doubtless have their own), and it too will change as men change. It will not change week by week of course, registering small and perhaps temporary ups and downs of mood. But a liturgy can come to be seriously out of contact with those who must use it: a period is seen to have ended. That is our position now. Changes have been made. Changes are in the air.

There are Catholics who view with alarm the likelihood of changes yet to be made in Mass and Communion. Mere custom has a way of ringing itself with a kind of sacredness which can pass for the real thing. Thus when the Eucharistic Fast was first reduced to three hours, there were those who still insisted upon fasting from midnight. Yet how much sense there was in the Pacific Islander who, having to walk long miles to Mass, ate a

MASS AND EUCHARIST 105

banana on the way and explained his reception of Communion by saying that it was more honorable for his Lord to sit on a banana than for a banana to sit on his Lord. Indeed there seems to be at least as good a case for fasting after Communion as before.

We are less likely to be alarmed at some of the changes we hear proposed if we realize what changes there have already been. I do not mean where the Church has had to forbid wrongful uses of the Sacrament—in the fourth century the Council of Hippo forbade giving the Host to the dead, and the practice persisted for a couple of hundred years after that. What I have in mind is the changing of practices not in themselves wrong. As late as 800 years after the Last Supper, it was normal for priests to place the Host in the communicant's right hand, the communicant kissing it and putting it into his own mouth. I have already referred to a recent unofficial revival of this practice. As late as the fourth century the laity were allowed to take Hosts home with them, receive them privately there, and administer them to others: which is as surprising to us as the visits to the Blessed Sacrament Catholics have been making for the last two centuries would have seemed to them.

Will we perhaps, like the Protestants, have Communion in both kinds—already allowed in a variety of circumstances (at Nuptial Masses, for instance) —for all Catholics at all Masses? Actually it is mere provincialism on our part to think of this as Protestant. Within our own Communion, linked like us to the Pope, nineteen (or is it twenty?) different middle-Eastern and Eastern Churches have it. The early Church had it—it also had the giving of Communion to babies in one kind, the Blood only, in the form of a drop on the tongue. No question of principle is involved.

We hold three facts in mind, two major, one minor. The major are that in receiving under *either* kind, there is nothing of Christ that we do not receive, so that we can receive no more of Him under both; and that the command to receive both was given to the men gathered round Christ at the Last Supper, who were themselves to offer the sacrifice. The minor is that Communion as we receive it, under the appearance of bread, has drawn to it such millions as the Church who administer the Chalice have never experienced.

A totally different question is being heard: should Sunday obligation be abolished as the Lenten Fast has been? I am thinking not of Catholics being given the choice of either Saturday or Sunday, but of whether obligation, or any sort of compulsion, has a place here. Most of us, I think, have not given much thought to the question.

But there are those who feel passionately about it. I have heard it urged that one should no more command a man to go to Mass than to get married —love should be the only motive for either. But that is to over-simplify.

Getting married is to be compared not with going to Mass but with becoming a Catholic, and compulsion would indeed be as monstrous in one as in the other. But each condition—being married, being a Catholic—carries with it certain obligations. A man should support his family out of love: but if he doesn't, the law will compel him, physically if necessary.

Out of love for Christ and our fellow-men, we

should join with them in offering the Mass. There is no question of physical compulsion; but should the Church make it a grave sin for us not to go to Mass on certain days? It is too complex a question for discussion here. When a particular action is a privilege beyond price—as to join with others in the worship of God certainly is—it may seem like mere legalism to remind ourselves that it may also be a duty.

Ideally we should need no urging, no reminder even, certainly no command. For in the Mass we unite with our Lord in His own worshipping, sacrificing, offering action, and make it ours, make its redeeming power ours. In the Mass we act as the "royal priesthood" we are, as the co-redeemers we are. Why should we have to be "obliged" to it?

But we must take ourselves as we find ourselves. Realization is our continuing problem. The great spiritual realities do not tug at us, solicit us, build up cravings in our bodily organisms as the world about us does. "Hunger and thirst after righteousness" does not mean parching in the throat or torment in the entrails. It would be easier for us if it did. We need the Mass, need it urgently, need it more than we need food and drink. But we do not *feel* the urgency in the same way, and plenty of us do not feel it at all.

Many a man is grateful that Sunday Mass is of obligation. Perhaps he cannot imagine staying away. But there were years when the obligation helped to get him there, and there are things the Mass can do to those who take part in it, no matter what brought them to it.

There may be changes that go deeper than any

we have glanced at. What we regard as the primary purpose of any institution must affect our attitude to it and all our judgements about it. We are seeing this in the matter of marriage, with procreation no longer holding its solitary pre-eminence. We are seeing the same principle in action, and we may well see it a great deal more in the matter of the Blessed Eucharist. Christ is really present; therefore He is to be adored. He is present in this special way in order that He may be received as food. Is adoration primary, or nourishment? We have glanced at this already; we may glance at it again from another angle.

For long the emphasis seemed to be on adoration: hence the infrequent reception—months of preparation regarded as essential—and the fast from midnight. What mattered was the communicant's *fitness* to receive the Adorable One within himself. We are now placing the emphasis where our Lord placed it: on nourishment. What matters most is the communicant's *need*. Where the one consideration used to be to safeguard the honor due to Christ, the whole mind of the Church now is to remove any obstacles in the path of those who need to be fed. Is the food reaching all who need it and could be nourished by it?

How far will this carry us? The question is already being raised about giving the Eucharist to baptized Christians not of our Church. Their need for Christ's Body is not less than ours; their love for Him is not less; is their willingness to receive the Sacrament, knowing what we mean by it, condition enough for reception? Permission, we know, has already been given in individual cases.

This matter will press itself on the Church's attention if the offering of Mass in private houses continues and increases—not as a substitute for the parish Mass in Church, but over and above. Might it be possible for the non-Catholic husband or wife who believes our Lord really present to receive Him with the rest of the family?

With Mass in private homes, indeed, we seem to have an echo of the Jewish Passover, at which the head of each family presided. Is there likely to be any revival, or development, of this liturgical role for the husband and father? If so there is, as we have seen, a certain hint of a precedent in the early Church.

All these questions are for the Church to decide. But it looks as if we may see a wider admission to Communion than we now know—unbelievers welcomed, perhaps even sinners who are at present barred. The question is being seriously asked whether we have been too protective of the dignity of the Sacred Host. Our Lord redeemed the world by submitting His body to publicans and sinners (Lk 7:46), even to those who hated Him or slew Him. Need the Church be more protective of it in its sacramental presence in which it still works for the redeeming of the world?

We have noted that St. Peter might not have found today's High Mass in St. Peter's easy to follow. But then, neither would that rather more recent Pope, Pius xii, perhaps.

And changes in the Liturgy—made and still to be made—are not the only sort. There are those who would be rid of vestments, because our Lord was wearing his street-clothes at the Last Supper.

So far, I think, only a minority see anything incongruous in putting color to use in the actual offering of the Mass; though I seem to notice that in ceremonial wear outside the Sanctuary scarlet and purple cause less excitement than of old. Pageantry is good—while men's hearts are made joyous by it; if they cease to be then it has outlived its usefulness.

Archbishop Mannix, the great Irishman who ruled the Diocese of Melbourne for fifty years, told me of a stranger who came up to him, pointed to his pectoral cross, and said "Christ was not crucified on gold and ivory." The Archbishop remained deep in thought after he had finished telling the story. I was reminded of this incident when at the Council the Latin-American Bishop Camara urged his fellow bishops to wear crosses made of wood.

In fact a simplification—in vestments, in church buildings, to say nothing of living standards—may be forced on us by something different from a mere change of taste. It may be more like a change of heart. For ourselves to live richly while—in India, say—every day thousands die of starvation is uncomfortable, unless we can manage to switch our minds from it (which we do fairly easily.) And to spend upon the glory of God money which might save from starvation all those thousands made in His image does not necessarily give him the glory He wants.

We remember St. Ambrose melting down the Church plate to get money to buy back from slavery Roman soldiers captured by the Goths after their victory at Adrianople. The Arians—heretics as it happened—accused him of sacrilege.

And he said "It is far better to preserve souls for our Lord than to preserve gold." When a man was found dead of starvation in a Roman street, Pope Gregory the Great fasted for days. And our own Pope has made clear that the poverty of the world must be a primary concern.

6

Ecumenism

1

Ecumenism is the word of the moment; the new friendliness between ourselves and other Christians is the fact of the moment. The Church of the future will be very much affected by what happens to ecumenism. For it is only in its feeble beginning, and might not survive. Plenty of men on both sides will have none of it.

Even the Catholics who rejoice in it are not easy in it yet. After all, we have had only ten years to grow into it. Nor are Christians of other Churches any easier with us. In our get-togethers we are pretty self-conscious—at any rate the first few times. We put on our party manners, watch our words, are careful to remind ourselves to be ecumenical —not exactly acting a part, but not relaxed and at ease either. When Isaiah tells of the wolf dwelling with the lamb and the leopard lying down with the kid, he does not tell us of a certain strain that cannot but be there the first time they try it. It is

113

worth asking ourselves why it should be so new, and feel so strange, for men who love Christ to come together naturally as friends.

When the lines were drawn after the Reformation, Catholics and Protestants were in agreement with about a good 80 per cent of the Christian revelation: Trinity, Incarnation, Redemption, the Moral Law, the World to Come. But from the beginning, their relations with each other were based not on this great treasure of truth shared, but on the 20 per cent about which they differed. (They differed not only from us, of course, but among themselves.) It was about the 20 per cent that they and we talked to each other, or rather shouted at each other, till the whole sky was filled with the shouting. A world which should have been won to Christ heard nothing of His message —only the quarrelling about the smaller part of it. Though love is the key to everything in the Christian religion, Christians seem unable to differ lovingly.

An Australian verse writer of my boyhood, W. T. Goodge, wrote a kind of parable about a Mohammedan who thought he would study Christianity. He gathered to his house representatives of a number of Christian religions. Within minutes they had forgotten him and were arguing with one another:

The United Presbyterian he ventured to
   suggest
That the doctrine of the Calvinists was better
   than the rest,
Which aroused the wrath and anger of the
   Plymouth Brother, who

Said he thought a Presbyterian no better than
a Jew.

When the Baptist made his statement with
much eloquence and force
He was flatly contradicted by the Anglican, of
course.
And the Quaker and the Shaker used some
language very strong,
But they both agreed in stating that the
Catholic was wrong.

—a judgement the Catholic had already passed
upon them.

When I first read this, I was undergoing an
experiment in Ecumenism myself—a unique experiment, I think. I tell it here because it affects
my whole attitude to other Churches, and indeed
to my own as well.

My mother was a Catholic, a Maloney from
County Limerick. My father was a Marxist. Whether
he believed in God I never discovered, but he was
against Churches. Priests and ministers of every sort
were "black-coated confidence men." The *Communist Manifesto* was his Bible. Every meal meant
a monologue by my father on Karl Marx. So far the
case is routine; but when I was eight—having already made my first Confession and Communion—
my father decided to send my young brother and me
three times every Sunday to the Methodist Church
in the next block.

And so for six years it happened: Marxism at
every meal, Methodism on Sundays, daily Mass
during the two weeks of my father's annual absence
from home on vacation. A heckler in Times Square

once told me that I believed in the Catholic Church because I had been brain-washed as a child: he hadn't a notion of how many competing detergents my small brain had been scrubbed with.

Looking back, I see that it was hard on the Methodists to have two children wished on them, who resented being forced to be there. We took no part in the service. I never sang a hymn: but I learned lots of hymns by heart and sang them to myself. I still do, in fact. That may be why the Gelineau Psalms depress me—they lack the life and vigor of the Methodist hymns of my boyhood; they seem to be a pious droning in comparison. I am not defending my taste in this matter, only admitting it.

I had gone there resentfully, but I came to like ministers and congregation individually and ended my six years with a great personal devotion to John Wesley, and with the feeling that, had I not known Catholicism, I'd have thought it a splendid thing to be a Methodist. Yet my Catholic faith was all the stronger for the experience.

I was particularly impressed by the fact that in all those years I had never heard a word against the Catholic Church. But one feeling remained constant—I was inside, they were outside. I'd have loved to have them all join the Catholic Church. But I never thought of this as a possibility. Reunion was not in the air then. Now that it is, it still seems to me if not impossible, at least wildly improbable.

Why? Is it just Catholic arrogance on my part? Evidently, no. The Protestant Churches have split from one another and stayed that way. It is not the Catholic Church which keeps them from reuniting. It is that they sincerely differ in what they hold to be God's will for men—what God wants us to believe; how He wants us to live.

There are two ways out. *Either* there might be a genuine change of mind leading to a general agreement upon what God wants men to hold. *Or* the importance attached to belief might diminish, with doctrine seen as not essential in religion. The second alternative may look the more promising of the two, especially today when voices are raised urging that love is what matters, as though we could change Augustine's great "Love, and do what you will" into "Love, and believe what you will," a development which would have horrified Augustine. There are even voices urging that religion can go right on with God himself omitted, as either non-existent or irrelevant; but those who talk like this (I shall discuss them later) are a small minority. For most Catholics, the second alternative is imposible. For most Protestants, I think, it is repellent.

Only the first way, a change of mind, is practical —in the sense that, if it *could* happen, it would solve the problem of reunion. But how impractical it sounds all the same, how unrealistic it would be to hope for it in any foreseeable future. Yet we know very well that, if God wills, words like "impractical" and 'unrealistic" are wind and no more. Let us look closely at our differences, enter into the most full and open dialogue about them, both with others and among ourselves. Some of these differences may be little more than verbal. But there are profound cleavages: upon these, men can but do their best to show what they hold and why they are convinced God wants them to hold it, and what their souls gain from holding it, each praying to God for the other. And for himself. It looks as if it will be a long job. We must make a beginning.

But if the union of minds seems to be a matter of the far future, there is another union which need not wait for it, namely the union of hearts. In the days when I was sent to the Methodist Church I did not know that John Wesley had said, in his wonderful *Letter to a Roman Catholic:* "If we cannot as yet think alike in all things, we can at least love alike."

In this order of Christian love Protestants have already made splendid progress with one another, but not with Catholics, nor Catholics with them. The slowness of each in the matter is caused by the Catholic Church's claim to be the one true Church. (Vatican ii reaffirms this at the beginning of the Constitution on the Church.) Protestants resent the claim, we resent their existence as a frustration of the claim. And resentment is an obstacle to love.

Is resentment too strong a word for the Catholic attitude to other Christians? Perhaps. I go back to my own attitude to the Methodists. As I have said, I regarded ourselves as inside and them as outside. It never occurred to me that they were in peril of damnation—the suggestion that only Catholics could be saved had never reached my ears. I was not worried about their eternal future, but I was sorry for them here and now, because they had not the Mass or the Real Presence of Christ in the Eucharist, because they had not the companionship with our Lady and St. Joseph and some of the other saints which meant so much to me.

I thought—and I fancy most of us thought like that until Pope John opened so many windows—that individual Protestants were good people, but not that the Church they belonged to might be a good thing. It did not occur to us of the Catholic rank and file to think that Protestant Churches were doing work which, in the present condition of the world, God wanted done, and that God would be pleased with them for doing it and give them grace to do it better.

I do not think that we denied these things. They simply never occurred to us. But in a single address at Christmas, 1958, Pope John changed all that. Of the various Christian bodies he said, "They bear the name of Christ on their forehead." Nothing could be the same after those words had been spoken. The union of minds might be in the far distance, but nothing stood between us and the union of hearts. Nothing, that is, but the hardness of our hearts. And theirs, of course. We must analyze that hardness.

2

In the days before Ecumenism we prayed for "our separated brethren": now we find our highest authority calling them simply "our brothers," and there is joy in the change. But is it more than a change of phrasing? After all, they *are* separated. Are we just trying to make *them* feel good? Or is the Church perhaps softening *us* up, getting ready to abate her own claim to uniqueness just as some want her to abate her claim to authority? Could it be that when Pope John said that the other Christian bodies "bear the name of Christ on their forehead," he was conceding them full equality?

To any of these questions we could give a plain yes or no. Yet the naked monosyllable might be misleading. More would need to be said, and I shall say it—or some of it. But the dropping of the word "separated," while separation still exists, is no empty gesture. It emphasizes brotherhood, and stops treating the separation as the first fact to be mentioned about so splendid a relation.

Meanwhile, separated we are. We differ as to the truths Christ wants men to hold; and the removal of that difference, whether by a discussion of each separate matter of disagreement, or by arriving at an agreed method of deciding how we are to know what Christ did in fact teach, looks like being a very long labor. The union of minds is evidently not just over the horizon. The union of hearts—building our relations with one another on the love of Christ common to us all—looks easier, and *is* easier. But it is not easy. There is too long a history of hostility. Of two disfigurements in ourselves, bigotry and prejudice, we and they alike must be cleansed.

I have never met a man who knew that he was a bigot. But most of us are, until we realize the fact and fight against it. Bigotry does not mean believing that those who disagree with us are in error—of two contradictory views, one must be wrong. Bigotry means believing that they must be dishonest. I remember a questioner who said to me, "Either you're paid to say these things or you're mentally deficient"—a moment later he went on, "I can't imagine anybody paying you." If on any serious matter we find someone not holding what we hold, our immediate instinct is to assume that he is either a fool or a knave: as time passes, he becomes a knave only. If we ourselves feel very strongly on the matter of our difference, dislike is practically inevitable, and dislike can turn to hatred. In the way of the union of hearts stands the hardness of men's hearts, and hardness is never harder than when it wears the mask of loyalty to our own Faith. A man can reach a condition in which he measures his love for his own cause by his hatred of the other.

Once we are aware of bigotry, we can fight against it and even conquer it. But prejudice is far more difficult to root out of ourselves. It is the tendency to judge exactly the same set of facts differently according to whether they are on our side or the other. It so permeates our mind's activity that it is immeasurably difficult to catch ourselves at it. An accusation is made against our side and we demand the most rigorous proof. A similar accusation is made against the other side and we accept it out of hand—it is just the kind of thing those people would do! Prejudice conditions our judgement. It conditions our memory too: we remember what they did to us in centuries past; we have forgotten what we did to them.

And in this matter they—I mean those of them who were strong enough to persecute—are not much better than we. They cast up at us the Protestants that the Catholic Queen Mary burnt at Smithfield; we come right back with the Catholics her Protestant sister had hanged, drawn and quartered at Tyburn. They talk of our burning Cranmer. We remind them that Cranmer was one of the judges who sentenced Thomas More to be beheaded, and we throw in Cranmer's burning of the Anabaptist, Joan Bocher, for good measure. And so it goes on.

Bigotry and prejudice are moral defects in us,

with mental weakness at their base. We strive against them, constantly examine our conscience about them. But there are other factors which make close relations difficult. Of these the chief is that we have been differently conditioned by the practice of different religions. Situations arise in which each finds the other incomprehensible. Thus the Protestant has always considered that ultimately he must make his own decisions, that there is no authority upon earth which has authority from God to tell him what he must believe or what he must do. The Catholic attitude to Church authority seems to him to be of a servility beyond comprehension, while to the Catholic his seems to verge on anarchy. But he is not an anarchist, nor are we servile.

I have mentioned only one of a dozen incomprehensions. Even now, in what we may call the honeymoon of Ecumenism, we and they can find ourselves feeling, if not like Isaiah's wolf and lamb, at least like people from different planets. And the honeymoon will not last. Honeymoons are not meant to. On each side men feel that sacred truths are being challenged. Not only that: the other man, whom one could answer so well in a pamphlet, proves maddeningly difficult to answer when he's actually there. We must prepare ourselves well in advance to hang on to our tempers whatever happens.

3

Is it the same Church? We may be clearer about that as our inquiry proceeds. Let us for the moment agree that it does not look quite the same, or feel quite the same. Ecumenism, even in its small beginnings—where it means only that the different Churches recognize one another as brothers in Christ, friends not enemies—has changed both the look and the feel. Yet how small the beginnings are, how difficult is the next stage to reach. Or even to see.

These first movements towards each other have had the paradoxical result of emphasizing the differences. The ordinary Protestant and the ordinary Catholic have for centuries known as little of each other as if they were from different planets. They got that way by having no habit of civil conversation about the things of God. When they were not shouting at each other, there grew up a sort of gentlemen's agreement not to talk about religion at all. The result is that on each side myths grew up about the other.

I think they have more myths about us than we about them. Protestantism is less spectacular, there is less in it to catch the eye. We have the Pope, for instance, a very eye-catching figure. He seems to concentrate Catholicism in himself as no single person concentrates any other Christian body. In all honesty a Protestant might think we put the Pope in place of God as no one has ever suspected the Eastern Orthodox of putting the Patriarch of Constantinople. The man who dreamed of the Pope and woke in a cold sweat screaming "Rome" is a caricature, of course, but everybody recognizes the type. Nobody, I think, ever dreamed of Archbishop Ramsey and woke in a cold sweat screaming "Canterbury."

I remember an old lady who listened to me lecturing on Papal Infallibility at a street corner meeting. At the end, she said, "It's no good: you can talk till you're black in the face. You'll never get me to believe that your Pope is God." I had not said it, of course; but she took for granted that Catholics believe it, and she drew the only possible conclusion from the fact that I had not denied it!

She was no intellectual, that one. But at all intellectual levels there is a failure to understand what the Papacy actually means in Catholic teaching. There is simply the myth, shapeless but sinister. John XXIII was seen as different—and different he was—not only from extremely unattractive nonentities like John XII but from towering Popes like Innocent III. In fact, there never has been a Pope in the least like him. He did not fit the myth. The feeling is growing that he was too good to be true!

But, largely because of him, Catholics and Protestants are beginning to meet not as fellow citizens but as brothers in Christ, with conversation no longer excluding the things of God. The myth will not survive. But to establish the reality we shall have a lot of explaining to do, not only to make clear what the doctrinal position is, in the abstract so to speak, but to show the Papacy as it lives and functions. And the true doctrine and the living reality may repel the mind of the non-Catholic even more than the myth shocked his moral sense.

That is what I mean by saying that a first result of our drawing closer is to emphasize the differences. It will happen with regard not only to the Papacy but to doctrine after doctrine, practice after practice: our Lady, Mass and Eucharist, Confession, Purgatory, Invocation of Saints. Again and again we'll have the experience of clearing away a myth and explaining what we really hold—only to find that they like the reality even less than the myth.

I know all about this—I have had forty-seven years of it on street corners, in university lecture halls, in inter-faith conferences. This is one of the key realities of Ecumenism, and it is not often discussed. When we and they get to know each other and really start talking, we shall often find the experience painful, even crucifying. But educational too—for ourselves, I mean. It is a kind of education not at present available to most Catholics. When one has done a lot of explaining of the Faith to people who can answer back, it may still be the same Church, but one is not the same Catholic—better, please God, but certainly changed.

For one thing we shall realize that we differ from Protestants not only about this and that doctrine or practice, but in the depths of our personalities. A man who believes and practices the Catholic Faith is almost living in a different universe from one who does not—so different a universe that he is almost a different species. Consider some of the differences. There is our acceptance of authority, not as a chain binding us but as an indispensable condition of freedom. There is our closeness to the dead, to the saints in Heaven and the saints-to-be in Purgatory. There is the whole great matter of Christ's Mother, with the certainty that she is our Mother too, which takes us on pilgrimage to Lourdes. There is the sometimes scarifying, seldom wholly agreeable, experience of the Confessional; and over and above all, creating the atmosphere we breathe all our Catholic life, we have Mass and the Blessed Eucharist.

All this is at once an environment conditioning the Catholic, and a life operative in him. He is different. A different species? Almost. Different, anyhow, recognizably different. Even if he has lost the Faith he is recognizable! The very blasphemy of a once-Catholic is different. Many times we of the Evidence Guild have recognized a fallen-away Catholic by his way of uttering his hatred of the Church. I don't mean only the use of Catholic phrases, or the recital of Catholic experiences, but something in the very shape of the mind. It is the result, I think, not only of what is ordinarily thought of as conditioning, but of the Mass and Sacraments, and of a still more profound result of the effect upon the soul's very substance of the grace that had once been there. Two cases come to mind, both hostile, one violently, one sneeringly. Our speakers were certain that both had been Catholics. They were right. One had been a nun, one a priest. These two returned to the Faith. Not all do.

But in the practicing Catholic the difference is more obvious. When we meet Protestants at the level of genuine conversation about religion, they and we feel the difference: a strangeness, let us call it. We are happy to be with them, we smile easily and they smile back. But so often they find us—as we find them—incomprehensible. The smile is still there, but the face has gone blank. The words are not getting through.

Meeting only our fellow-Catholics we find no need to explain these things—either the doctrines or practices of the Church, or ourselves as conditioned by them. But there can be loss for ourselves in this. Having no need to explain them, we had no need to examine them. And frequently they would be better for examination. Mental, moral and emotional habits grow in us that are not rooted in reality but in earlier habits, and these again in still earlier ones. We examine our conscience, but our whole religious mind needs examining occasionally to check its contents against Reality. This sort of examination is forced on us by ecumenical conversation. At last we are meeting with other Christians as brothers in Christ who have great things in common but matters of difference, too. Conversation will no longer exclude the things of God; the gentlemen's agreement to exclude them will be seen as a rather grotesque period-piece.

We shall have a lot of explaining to do, and that will be good, because to explain we must examine. Take the Mass, for instance. We equip ourselves to tell our friends about it. We tell them, we meet their reactions. Our own Mass becomes a new experience ever after. Their reactions will give us light or drive us to search for light. I have gained more from my outdoor hearers than they ever gained from me, I fear. Of this kind of examination—of our doctrines and of ourselves and of other minds —we have at present no habit, and it will bring some surprises. Errors will come to light which we had been taking for granted all our lives. Some myths about Protestants will be destroyed, and rich elements in doctrine will be discovered for the first time.

And it is not only we who will be surprised: our clergy will find that we have become a new laity. Catholics who know the truths of revelation and are alive to them will make a very different congregation to preach to, a very different parish to cooperate with. We shall be able to bring them news of other Christian groups which will enrich their own approach.

None of what has been said so far means that it will become a different Church. It will be the same Church but in better health. There is a solid pleasure in Ecumenism as the first green shoots begin to show above the ground: Catholics and Protestants meeting as brothers in Christ, as friends not enemies. But it carries a temptation with it. Many temptations, actually, but one in particular.

4

Consider what the situation was. It is not so long since that there were Catholics who thought Pius IX was selling the pass when he allowed the possibility that Protestants mght be saved. And it seems only yesterday that I heard Protestants calling the Pope the beast of Revelation, and the Church the Scarlet Woman. There was the Anglican Dean of St. Paul, Dean Inge, an intensely civilized man. I once spent a most agreeable weekend with him as a fellow guest of the poet, Alfred Noyes. Phrases written by him stay in my head—he wrote of "the lucrative imposture of Lourdes," he flipped the Church aside as "A harassed and dwindling minority by the shores of the Mediterranean Sea." He was astounded when Catholics objected to his description of their Church as "a bloody and treacherous corporation"—he thought they knew it!

These attitudes still survive, if vestigially. On both sides men are warning ecumenically-minded friends "Watch out, they'll stab you in the back." But the general shape of things has altered out of recognition. At all levels there are friendly meetings and enjoyment in them. The new situation is all the more agreeable by contrast with what preceded it. Euphoria wraps us round. There is real luxury in it. But there is no luxury without danger.

In its simplest form, there is the instinctive dislike of spoiling an agreement we find so pleasant. Protestant friends speak as if on some point our view is the same as theirs, when it very definitely is not. We decide to let it pass, not from any desire to delude, but simply not to break the spell. So we seem to be assenting when in fact we are merely being polite: the result is that they think we are closer than we are: a point arises at which we really should speak our difference. I don't mean that we should argue it but merely inform them of it. We have made it almost impossible to do so.

All this is natural; there is no evil anywhere in it. But there is a graver danger, and it is already showing itself, the danger of making Ecumenism an end in itself—with what the Church is to say or do judged, not by its own truth, but by whether it will help or hinder the growing together of all Christians into one. It is something like Karl Marx's teaching that the only rule of morality, the only test of right or wrong action, was whether it helped or hindered the Proletarian Revolution.

There are two levels of this "ecumenical" standard of what is right or wrong to teach. One, less common, is a desire to change the doctrines or practices themselves in order to eliminate differences; we shall consider this later. The other makes a principle of the instinct I have already mentioned —to talk only of points of agreement and be silent about the rest, not changing our teachings but soft-pedalling some of them in the interests of unity.

There was an incident of this sort forty years ago, told me by one who was present at the conversations between Catholics and Anglicans held at Malines under Cardinal Mercier. For some time the discussion had proceeded on the authority of the Papacy, and it was felt that the two groups were drawing steadily closer, reducing difference almost to a pinpoint. Then one of the participants—later to be a Cardinal—raised the question of Christ's godhead; and the appearance of unity vanished.

There were many at that time who felt that he should not have raised the question. We hear a similar irritation expressed now at any assertion that the Catholic Church is the Church that Christ founded, any mention of the unique honor we owe the Mother of God, any teaching on the Mass as Sacrifice.

I am not talking now of those theologians who want real "correction" of the Church's present teachings on Our Lady, and the Mass, and the Church itself. My present concern is with the view that Ecumenism is best served by postponing the evil day when the differences must be brought out into the open. At present, they say, it is "inopportune." That, to me, is *the* temptation which the splendid upsurge of Ecumenism has brought with it. It is even more likely to destroy Ecumenism than its opposite, the impulse to argue every difference, especially by people on either side who lack the necessary knowledge. If we yield to the temptation of silence, we really will have a different Church —different in its relation to God.

Catholics can actually damage the cause of that Ecumenism which they rightly love so ardently by a determination to leave in the background the great matters on which our Church differs from others. Why, they ask, did Pope John *have to* insert St. Joseph into the Canon of the Mass? Why did Pope Paul *have to* declare our Lady's motherhood of the Church? Why did the Declaration of Religious Liberty *have to* insist that the Catholic Church is the one true Church?

It is not that they themselves find any difficulty in these things. There are, of course, those who do. Let us take the third: one knows theologians who wish to discard the phrase "One true Church" as a formula we should have outgrown. I have already mentioned the Jesuit and the Benedictine who urged that contented Protestants had better not become Catholics but remain ecumenically where they were. These do want a real "correction" or modification of the Church's present teaching about itself: so perhaps do the Catholics who cry out as if we had touched an exposed nerve when we suggest that there is any advantage whatever in being a Catholic!

But I am speaking here of the Catholics whose abiding fear is that we should make any statements that will widen the breach between ourselves and Protestants. "Inopportune," I have noted, is the key-word. But the one test of whether a statement should be made is whether it is true. The only reason why any man, Catholic or Protestant, should hold any doctrine is a conviction that it is from God. If he is sure that it is, how can he withhold it from others? "Preach the word," says St. Paul, "in season and out of season." The truth has no closed season. If truths are from Christ, they are nourishment for the soul. A man cannot be happy while others are starving for food he is convinced Christ wants them to have. This implies no personal judgement of these others. They may be holier than he, love Christ more, be more loved by Christ. But if he has bread that they have not, he will want to share it with them.

I am as ecumenical as most. I rejoice in the union of hearts, pray for the union of minds, am glad that these other Christian groups are taking Christ our Lord to men who, for whatever reason, will not accept Him from us. But when I meet a Baptist—say—I want him to have all that my Faith has given me. And, if the Baptist is the man I hope he is, he feels the same way about me.

What lies behind the desire to play down differences? Partly the feeling that the union of hearts, so newly come into existence, must not be imperilled. Partly from the associations connected with "sitting round a table," each side prepared for a reasonable give-and-take: in religion no one would consciously argue like that. But don't let us underrate our own subconscious.

In fact, a little reflection would show that this line cannot serve, but only disserve, Ecumenism. It ignores Psychology—man's, and, if one dare phrase it so, God's.

Human psychology it ignores in two ways. First it is certain to end in disappointment—postponing the evil hour means that when the hour does come it will be worse, because of the hopes our silence has allowed to grow. One must not only assert unwelcome truths but keep on asserting them. Once is not enough! Countless people now are genuinely resentful because they had assumed that Pope John was promising a diminution of Catholic claims, which he did not promise and could not have promised. Nothing is more maddening than the feeling of having been led up the garden path.

The second ignoring of human psychology bears upon the nature of religious conviction. At present Catholics and Protestants are held from union by genuine differences as to what God wants men to believe and how He wants them to act. The union of minds can be served only by clarity—clarity possessed by each, clarity shared with the other. Each *must* know the fullness of what the other holds, otherwise the real discussion which might bring them closer is impossible. The best service we can render them, and they us, is to speak freely and listen attentively.

And there must be no resentment at opinions honestly held. I know of a town in which the Catholic bishop and the Anglican bishop are the closest of friends, on Christian name terms. The Catholic does not believe in the validity of the other's Orders. The other regrets that his friend should be mistaken about this, but does not let the "mistake" dim the friendship or impede the work they can do together for the service of the Lord they both love.

I have spoken of an ignoring of God's "psychology"—it lies in forgetting the part that must be His in the realm of Faith. What matters is what will please God, not what will please the other party. And God is not served by diplomacy. We have had a notable illustration in the Definition by Pope Pius XII of the dogma of our Lady's Assumption into Heaven. There were plenty, on both sides, who felt that this was the last straw. They could not imagine anything which would drive Catholics and Protestants further apart. That was in 1950. Seven years later we had Pope John. Catholics and Protestants are now closer together than ever in their history. God came into action. To say nothing of our Lady.

5

However clearly and honestly we speak our minds, a Catholic back after ten years on a desert island would find that our attitude to other Christian Churches has changed fantastically; Rome was never like this, he would feel.

Take one single matter. In all the hundreds of pages of Constitutions and Declarations of the Second Vatican Council, I cannot remember meeting the words "anathema" or "heretic" or "excommunication." That, you feel, might be simply politeness, a change indeed, but only in manners. For the three words do express realities: after all, Paul used the first two, putting plenty of bite into each, and he excommunicated the incestuous Corinthian (1 Cor 5:2). Nor should we forget that our Lord said (Mt 18:17) of one who would not accept an "ecclesial" decision: "Let him be to you as the heathen and the publican," which is roughly what anathema means. And into His mouth the book of Revelation (3:16) puts the words, "Because you are neither hot nor cold I will spew you out of my mouth," which is the ultimate in excommunication.

If the non-use of such words were no more than politeness, that would still be a welcome change in religious discussion. But more it evidently is: it is a clear admission that the words do not apply to the other Churches. It is a simple application of the phrase with which Pope John signalled the end of an epoch: "They bear the name of Christ on their forehead."

Then are they members of Christ's Mystical Body? This, for many, has become the test of the sincerity of the Church's new friendliness to Protestants. If the answer is no, then our Ecumenism is a pretence, they feel, a smiling mask covering the same old arrogant power-greedy face. Our instinct is to answer yes—and that was so even before Pope John had used his great phrase. The Church had said clearly that men of other communions could be saved: therefore they can have sanctifying grace, which can come to men only because of Christ's redeeming sacrifice. And we had met Protestants who gave us an overwhelming sense of holiness, of a love and knowledge of our Lord beyond the level we were used to. It would seem like bigotry's last stand to say that they are not members of the Mystical Body.

Yet the Church has not said that they are. Pius XII's encyclical *Mystici Corporis* almost says that they are not—almost, I say: they are not *reapse* members. *Reapse* is a rare Latin word, meaning "in the full sense" or "in very fact": whatever the exact meaning, it modifies the word "not," leaving it more than flat negative. Nor does the Vatican Council go beyond the Encyclical's statement that they are "related" to the Church. "Men who believe in Christ and have been properly baptized are brought into a certain, though imperfect, communion with the Catholic Church" (*Ecumenism* 3). The same document goes one stage further: "Whatever is wrought by the grace of the Holy Spirit in the hearts of our separated brethren can contribute to our own spiritual up-building" (4).

But the Decree on Ecumenism does introduce a new element into the discussion: "All those justified by faith through Baptism are incorporated into Christ. They therefore have a right to be honored by the title of Christians" (3; and more strongly in 22). It seems as if a distinction is drawn between incorporation into Christ and incorporation into His Mystical Body. And we know that much thinking is being done by theologians upon the position of those who by baptism were made members of the Church, and though they have remained in their own Communions, have not deliberately separated themselves from it. It seems certain that a further statement will be made.

Meanwhile let us look more closely at the problem for ourselves. Membership of the Mystical Body is not a reward for virtue: it is not an honor to which men who love God are entitled; it is a function, implying work to be done. We find something similar in the Old Testament. There were holy Gentiles, God-loving Gentiles: but they were not members of the Chosen People. That people was not chosen for a privilege but for a function—to bear witness that there is one God, to prepare for the coming of Christ. And it was recognizable—the world knew it, its members knew one another. One was either a member of it, by birth or by a ritual entry, or one was not. It was not holiness that decided the matter of membership.

Christ has a Mystical Body, as He had a natural body, because He needs it for the work He has to do. The point of a body is that all the cells live with one life, the life of the person whose body it is: in the Church, all the members are in the stream of the life of Christ, whose Body it is. If that were all, why should not everybody, Christian or Jew or whatever, be a member, if he is in a state of grace?

But that is not all. As we have already reminded ourselves, my body does not exist to serve its cells: it exists to serve me. Christ has taken to Himself this second body because He has work to do in it. The question for every one of us is not "Am I as a cell getting all that's coming to me?" but "Am I as a cell helping Christ to do the work He took a body to do?"

A given non-Catholic may love God and his neighbor more than any number of given Catholics. But his conscience may compel him to speak against and work against truths we believe our Lord wants taught—the redeeming sacrifice of the Mass, the Real Presence of our Lord in the Blessed Eucharist, Trinity or Incarnation, Virgin Birth or Resurrection, even the Doctrine of the Mystical Body! It is hard to reconcile this "working against" with membership of a Body, hard to see how groups of Christians, sincerely contradicting one another in His name, fit into the reality of the Body.

And yet . . . .

7

Ecumenism and Our Lady

1

Between ourselves and other Christians there have been dozens of differences, a whole mountain chain of them, but I think there were three high peaks —the Mass, the Pope, and the Mother of Christ our Lord. And now, with Ecumenism in the air we breathe, the discussion is complicated to the point of shapelessness by what sounds like a break in Catholic certainty on all three. We have spoken at some length of the Mass (with Catholic voices urging that it is a meal only and no sacrifice) and of the Pope (with a professor's voice at a Catholic university wishing he would "keep his ——— hands off things"). What of our Lady?

When the dust of the Reformation battle had settled, she was a testing point—if you loved her, you were almost certainly a Catholic. I do not mean that no Protestants loved her; some did warmly. Nor do I mean that Protestants hated her, though there were some who seemed to come close;

again and again there was a virulence in the tone
and sometimes even the words used about her.
Chesterton called it "The little hiss that only comes
from hell."

But neither love nor hate was the ordinary
Protestant note; when I try to describe that "note,"
I wonder if the point is rather that there wasn't
any note, but rather an uneasy silence, a tendency
not to look very often or very closely at Christ's
mother, almost as if she were not there. Why should
this have been? They knew that she was the
mother of God's Son; every time they said the
Apostle's Creed they affirmed it. How, under heaven,
could she have become a symbol of division?

The answer which leaps to mind is that Protestants were reacting against Catholic exaggerations.
Exaggerations of course there were. In the Middle
Ages, to take one example, someone thought up the
idea that a certain group of elements from Mary's
body remained unchanged in her Son's, so that we
receive her, too, in the Eucharist: but after all it
was a Pope, Benedict xiv, who called this "fatuous."
With my own ears I have heard it said that, at the
Judgement, Mercy is represented by our Lady—
which would mean that if Infinite mercy should fail
us, we can always fall back on finite mercy! Upon
all this sort of thing Cardinal Newman uttered the
ultimate judgement—we do not honor the Mother
of God by saying things which can be explained
only by being explained away.

But many things that sound like exaggerations
are not so in fact. There is a language of human
love which makes sense only to those who share
the love. When a man says to a girl "I adore you,"
she does not reply primly, "Adoration is due to

God alone." She knows this, and knows that he knows it: her one desire is that he should tell her again that he adores her! But just as a man does not talk *about* his wife as he talks *to* her, we must tell our fellow Christians what our Lady means—not only to us but in herself—without rhetoric, without exuberance of affection. The exaggerations, in any event, are not the deepest reason.

We are face to face with a difference not primarily doctrinal—if it were that, it would be easier to discuss because it would be easier to say. The difference goes deeper; it is a "feel," something we have grown into and they have not. We have noted that living the Catholic life and living the Protestant life have produced almost two species. Unless that is grasped by both sides Ecumenism will make slow progress. Our habits are different, our reactions are different, our instincts different. And our Lady challenges the differences at so many points.

There is, for instance, her continuing interest in our life here and now. We have a matter-of-fact awareness of saints as citizens of one world with ourselves—in the Mass we ask the saints, whom we on earth honor, to intercede for us in heaven. Again, we do not count upon or readily accept miracles or visions, but we are not embarrassed by them, and would find it faintly surprising if they never happened at all. Men not similarly conditioned cannot "see" our Lady as we see her.

And then, of course, there is her virginity. Virtue is only secondarily the absence of sin; primarily it is the right direction of energy: and the energy thus rightly directed in virginity is the energy of love, given wholly to union with God and to doing

His will, direct, not through husband or wife. But this is no more known to the typical Protestant than to the Old Testament Jew. As a consequence, the statement in Matthew's Gospel and Luke's, and in the Apostles' Creed, that Christ was born of a virgin, seems utterly pointless.

So we have a bishop of another Christian body saying, "If Christ chose to be born of a virgin it's OK by me." He was flipping the Virgin Birth aside. But he had stated the decisive principle— *if Christ chose.* And in that principle lies the answer to certain Catholics who are asking loudly if she is any longer relevant. What *did* Christ choose?

I have a friend who holds that Christ not only should have been, but probably was, born of a woman of evil life. Only then would He have been sharing the human lot at its worst: to be born of a sinless mother, says my friend, would have meant that He was starting off with an unfair advantage over the rest of men.

I mention this odd view as an example of a tendency, from which even the devout are not free, to reconstruct our Lord's life as they think it ought to have been—as they would have lived it had they been the God-man. My friend's "reconstruction" in one direction is balanced in the other by the too frequent Catholic pictures of Joseph as an aged man. One sees how the idea grew up. There had to be a husband to stop the Jewish neighbors talking at the time; he had to be a very old man to stop Christians talking ever since!

Seen thus, Joseph was a mere convenience to save Mary's reputation, with no personality of his own, no part to play in the life of Mary or the upbringing of the boy Jesus. But for too many, Mary has been a mere convenience to get Christ born, of no further significance—as though God the Son, deciding to become man and noticing that men are born of mothers, said, "I suppose I'd better have one, too." The extreme Protestant refusal to take her into account implies this. The strange new voices among Catholics, which ask if she is any longer "relevant," imply it too.

Indeed, it seems to me that both imply something more. For no one can doubt that a man's mother is relevant to the man himself: Christ's mother must have mattered, can never cease to matter, to Christ. If she does not matter to us, then we must look more closely at our relation to Him. How real to us is Christ?

2

The future of Ecumenism may turn more upon this question than upon any of those matters now looming so large in inter-faith discussions. There are two movements of thought which bring Christ's reality into a different perspective.

There are those who hold that the "meaning" of the Gospel story is all that matters: love, mercy, the willingness to die for others—these are equally valuable whether nor not the Gospel incidents ever happened. They open up new horizons to us, implant in us new attitudes of life; they change our lives, and that—say the champions of this view —*is* redemption. Think, they say, of what the parables—the Good Samaritan, the Prodigal Son— have done in men's souls, yet the characters are strictly fictional: similarly the Gospel values are still there even if Christ has no more real existence than the men of the parables. It is not that they deny His existence; they simply think it of secondary interest: and His mother of less interest still—who cares about the Good Samaritan's mother?

It won't stand up, of course. It is not the Gospel message that has changed men's lives, it is Christ. "I live, now not I," says St. Paul, "but Christ lives in me." Try saying that with "the Prodigal Son," or "the Good Samaritan," or even "the Gospel message" substituted for "Christ."

And it won't fit what Christ came to do—to give His life, to pour out His blood for the remission of sins. That is what He Himself thought redemption meant. He came not only to teach but to do something, and a fictional Christ could do it only fictionally—which means that it would not be done and we would not be redeemed. "If Christ is not risen," says St. Paul, "we are the most miserable of men."

Which brings us to the second movement of thought which forces us to consider the meaning of our Lord's reality—a movement older, more orthodox, but devitalizing. For men of this mind, redemption is a kind of diagram, or the solution of a strictly legal problem. The state into which man had fallen required God to become man and die. But Redemption becomes almost an interplay of definitions—Christ fulfilled the definition of God and the definition of man: the flesh and blood details, that is the flesh and blood realities, were extras.

But the work of salvation was not a parable and not a formula. God the Son became not simply man, but that particular man, and the whole of his manhood was in redemptive action—body and blood, mind and heart, emotions and instincts, loves and repulsions. They were not extras, they poured their energies into our redemption: He offered them all—which means that He offered Himself as He was—to his Father. Nothing that mattered to Him can ever be irrelevant to us. And Mary of Nazareth was His Mother. For Catholics and for Protestants the challenge is to see Christ's Mother aright—*we* must correct any defects in our seeing, *they* must use the full power of their eyes upon her. In other words we must all of us use our minds upon her.

3

Too many Catholics decided to leave the thinking to the theologians while they themselves get on with the loving. And preachers have been known to let the head lie still while the heart ran riot, and the tongue outran the heart. As a reaction, Protestants too often developed an insensitiveness towards her (for many she survived only in Christmas carols). The conviction that we gave her too much honor strangely kept them from asking whether they themselves gave her enough.

And now we find a good many Catholics, too, reacting away from her for the same reason— revulsion against too much sugar. For Catholics of this mind, the decision of the Council to treat of our Lady in the Constitution on the Church mattered intensely—they felt, and said, that if she were given a separate Constitution to herself, the Council would have failed. It did not seem to me so crucial, for in *Theology and Sanity*, twenty years before, I had treated of Christ's Church and Christ's Mother in one chapter. I could as easily have given her one to herself. The point is to look straight at her.

She matters *because of* the Son she bore—a fact forgotten by a preacher we once heard who, having lavished all his oratory in praise of her virtues, concluded "And what must the Son of such a mother have been?" But she matters not only, or mainly, because she bore Him. What He did for her is greater than what she did for Him. He received His natural life from her; but she received her supernatural life and her eternal salvation from Him. Consider what St. Augustine wrote over 1500 years ago. "Mary was more exalted by her sanctity than by her motherhood of our Lord"; "More blessed was Mary in receiving Christ's faith than in conceiving Christ's flesh." Her entry into His Mystical Body meant more to her than His birth from her natural body. The last words we hear her say are "Do whatever he tells you" (Jn 2:5 [RSV]).

Upon the facts about her all Christians should base their own relation to her, whether or not other Christians seem to have got their relation twisted! All must have some beginning of the love and reverence her Son and our Savior must feel— must feel that is, unless He is utterly inhuman. Other Christians need not have our special devotions. But some devotion all should have, and some way of showing it. In a general way, even Protestants who find it hard to feel at home with her would agree with me. It is not easy, I admit, to imagine the Bishop of Such and Such, or Dean So and So, showing their love for her in any spectacular way. But my conviction is that most

Protestants could develop a true love for her, a true reverence, and know themselves closer to Christ for it.

But what of her motherhood *of us?* Lifelong Catholics take it in their stride, yet without giving any special thought to it. If we are to help Protestants to understand ourselves, and her, we had better think hard. She is a mother in the order of grace, of holiness to be sought by us and preserved from loss and regained when lost. And with this we come to a difference which runs very deep, almost down to bedrock, between the Catholic mind and the Protestant mind. That we should ask our Lady and the saints to care for us, pray for us, seems to Catholics the most natural result of Christ's redeeming work; to Protestants a plain denial of it. What can men do, they ask, that Christ cannot? As it happens, upon this matter Scripture is with the Catholic. Our Lord who is the Good Shepherd appointed Peter to be *Shepherd* (Jn 21:16–17). He is the Rock of Ages, but actually He made Peter the *Rock* on which He should build His Church (Mt 16:18). He is Savior, but Paul could write of himself as savior—"I became all things to all men, *that I might save all*" (I Cor 9:22); and he calls on Timothy to do likewise (I Tim 4:16).

Christ is the one Mediator: Paul (I Tim 2:1–5) gives that as the reason why we *should* help others by our prayers—help them to piety and chastity and so to salvation. And if *our* prayers can help them—in virtue of Christ's mediation—how much more can hers.

4

Our Lady is an acid test for ecumenism. Almost all the fundamental differences, which Catholics and Protestants must settle if re-union is to be thinkable, come to a point in the Catholic attitude to her.

That we should love her and reverence her is more and more clearly seen by all as involved in our imitation of Christ. That we should ask her prayers for divine help that we may do God's will and obtain salvation—and this is the essence of her motherhood—we can reasonably hope to show. For it comes within the general principle—which we have seen as scriptural—that all are called upon to take their part in applying Christ's redeeming plan to the souls of men.

But what of dogmas like the Immaculate Conception and Assumption, which are not mentioned in Scripture? Must we be content with a live-and-let-live compromise—they raising no objection to our believing them if we feel we must, we soft-pedalling them in interfaith conversation? I think we cannot. What is involved is the very nature of the Church; we cannot become one Church while we and they differ as to what the Church is.

The two dogmas are certainly not stated in Scripture, nor are they by any mathematical logic deducible from truths that Scripture does state. But by what we may call an organic logic they are there. Living the truths given to the Apostles by Christ, the Church grew to see that they implied certain other truths—if *this* is so, it is quite unthinkable that *that* should not be so. Thus if Mary is Christ's mother it is unthinkable that He should not have given her every gift of grace that she would want and He could give. If it is a penalty for sin that men must await the resurrection of their bodies, it is unthinkable that she, the sinless, should not be in heaven now, body and soul. In each of these two instances, by living the first truth the Church arrived at the certainty of the second.

This is not the logical certainty that a mathematician has, and can communicate, of the properties of a triangle. It is more like the certainty that a sailor has, but cannot convey to a landsman, of the sea; the certainty that a farmer has, but cannot demonstrate to a sailor, of the soil.

For Catholics, the Church is a living thing with a life principle by which, Christ aiding, it "tests all things," rejecting (not always instantly) things that do not serve its life, and absorbing, or making its own, the things that do. Upon acceptance or rejection of that view of the Church everything turns.

The Protestant, in the past, has not seen the Church so, though many are beginning to see it so now. The Catholic in the past *felt* the Church so, but had not used his mind upon it, had not analyzed it or stated it so, even to himself. The result is that many Catholics are rejecting it; never having actually seen it; the feeling, not rooted in understanding, has for great numbers simply faded away.

5

The more we think of our Lady, the harder we find it to fit her into Ecumenism. By "we" I don't mean the theologians on one side or the other, but the mass of Catholics and Protestants, the nobodies-in-particular—the majority, in fact. At the Reformation we were all Catholics; but as we have several times had occasion to note, in centuries of living apart religiously, they and we have become almost different species. And Mary of Nazareth focusses the difference in a quite unique way. Try to imagine, after the most ecumenical tea-party, telling your Protestant friends that she is their mother: you can see the glazed look come into their eyes, their desire to be ecumenical fighting against total incomprehension. Actually you would not do it: what, you ask yourself, would be the point? But be honest: are you dead sure you'd have the nerve?

Try it sometime. You needn't start by telling your friend she's *his* mother. You may very well be breaking the ice by mentioning her at all! If you decide to do that, I suggest that you do two things (1) ask Mary to help you (2) clarify your own mind about her motherhood of us. She is not our mother in the natural order, as she was Christ's, but in the order of grace. And in that order it was not she who conceived and bore us: He who was the source of grace in her is its source in us.

She is our Mother, says the Church, because Christ gave us to her and she accepted the gift. "We your children," says the prayer for the Conversion of England, "whom you received and accepted at the foot of the Cross." When He gave her as Mother to St. John, the words need strictly have meant no more than that: but they may have been spoken to John as a man, applicable to any man, to every man. And so for the best part of a thousand years the Church has seen them and Catholics have lived them.

She is our Mother by adoption—which does not diminish her motherhood. It is by adoption that we are God's children: His adoption of us is mightier than hers, but neither is fiction. And her motherhood of us is in the order of salvation, for it was given from the Cross, where every word was a ritual word, an element in the sacrifice which redeemed our race.

Thirty or forty years ago there was a cleric not of our fold who referred contemptuously to a statue of our Lady and the infant Jesus as "a female figure with a child." Hilaire Belloc wrote a ballade with that phrase for refrain. In three stanzas he excoriated the cleric: but in the Envoi his mind moved forward to the hour of his own death:

> Prince Jesus in mine agony
> Permit me broken and defiled
> Through blurred and glazing eyes to see
> A female figure with a child.

He was writing poetry, of course, not a theological examination paper. But the Catholic only has to hear that prayer to pray it with him.

Ecumenism is not a drawing together of doctrines or ceremonies, but of people. The problem is to bring into brotherhood people who love our Lady as their Mother and people who don't. Brotherhood is harder when there is that sort of difference about a Mother!

Catholic and Protestant have lived in two different worlds, and the Catholic lives mentally in the larger of the two. Whether the Catholic world is real or illusion may be matter for question: but what is beyond question is that there is more of it. The next world is closer to us, we are continually aware of it as active in ours, in living touch with ours, interpenetrating it. We are conscious of our own dead most especially, we know about the saints in general and have a personal devotion, a sense of a personal relation, to some of them. It does not occur to us that, in direct contact with their Creator and ours, they would have no further interest in their fellow-men on earth, that the second of Christ's commandments would have become a dead leter to them—any more than it is to Him.

In the world thus seen our Lady has her place and function as a matter of course. In that world many Christians, I think, do not live mentally. Catholics do. Or do they? The Church does. The whole of her liturgy is the hymn of two worlds interpenerating, one life throughout. But voices are heard of Catholics questioning it, questioning its reality, questioning at least its relevance.

We are back at the crisis of faith. And it is on a considerable scale. Nobody, I imagine, foresaw this as a sequel to the Council, with its splendid asseveration of the unity and orthodoxy of the Church, its surprising openness to advance into a future not yet charted.

In the excitement of those days Catholics almost forgot how tiny a section of mankind is concerned in Ecumenism, how vast a mass of mankind remains untouched by the Gospel—we of the street corner apostolate had no chance to forget it, our crowds having no more interest in the Vatican Council than in the World Council of Churches. However dark the world situation, the Council looked as if it might be a magnificent sunrise. Perhaps it was. But unless the Church can cope with the crisis of faith within her own body, the Council may prove to have been a sunset. The effect of magnificence proves nothing either way. One remembers Francis Thompson's line on the setting sun:

Thou dost thy dying so triumphally.

Sunset, of course, would not mean the end. There would be night, and a new dawning: we have Christ's confidence to support our own.

For myself, I do not see the present as sunset. With all the ominous cracks and fissures within our own Church, there is new hope. We must discuss this at more length later, always remembering that where God is concerned human calculations of probability cannot be decisive. The wind of the Spirit can blow the worst of them away like so many straws. Is that wind blowing now? Who can be sure? In parts of the Church some very odd winds are blowing gustily. If you throw the windows open, as Pope John did, you never know what will blow in.

8

How Living
Is God?

1

How much easier Ecumenism would be if only
there were two sets of beliefs, a Catholic and a
Protestant, with men on both sides striving to
narrow the gap between. Why, we ask in a pained
voice, why aren't Protestants like us? That there
is no Protestant unanimity of that sort is obvious;
it would be hard to name any one doctrinal statement upon which all Protestants would be of one
mind, in that it would be interpreted in the same
sense by all. Yet there *is* a Protestant mind, and
Protestantism is a Christian reality.

What about Catholics? Ten years ago there
could have been only one answer. There was
indeed a Catholic set of doctrines; there were
matters not yet settled of course, and controversies
which eddied and even boiled: the brotherliness
of Jesuits and Dominicans, for instance, was assumed to be of the Cain-and-Abel variety, all about
some doctrinal point beyond the reach of most of

us. But there was a vast body of doctrine to which the Church had definitely committed herself.

Catholics knew this. If they did not accept it, they simply dropped out. Officially that is still the position. All the Council documents assume it; no statement of Pope or hierarchy varies from it. Yet things are not the same. There really is a crisis of faith, though the Vatican Council did not discuss it. There are two main elements in it. The dropping out continues, perhaps at an accelerated pace. What is new is the number of Catholics who hold themselves free to differ from Pope and Council but do not drop out.

The first element, the falling away, we shall discuss at length later: we must balance against it the effect of the congregation's share in the vernacular Mass—which means that those who do stay in are closer than they have ever been to the uttered mind of the Church at its deepest. We cannot read the future: the falling away might grow to a flood, and the Church be reduced everywhere—might dwindle very much indeed. She would have to re-think her redemptive functioning. Yet she could still be the same Church.

Whereas if she accepts the presence within her of men who deny teachings to which she has committed herself, she will not.

To the ordinary Catholic there seems nothing particularly new about picking and choosing one's religious beliefs: he has known it all his life: it's Protestantism, isn't it? It looks like that, certainly. Indeed, when I hear Catholics—not laity only— deriding doctrines and practices they have held and taught all their lives, I seem to be hearing a voice I've known this forty years on the outdoor platform. It is the no-Popery voice of that strange Protestant underground, or undergrowth, the Protestant Alliance of England, which has so often shouted me down.

Yet in so many of the men who are differing from the Faith of their Fathers we do find a desire to stay with the Church, a conviction that they are serving, indeed preserving, the Church. And this needs closer examination. It affects only a minority so far. But, unchecked, it could spread. And how check it? Only by teaching the truth clearly and with conviction, not as against those who differ but in itself, yet in full awareness of the lines of difference. But where can this be done? Not in the pulpit at Mass, certainly: it would not fit very well with the offering of the Sacrifice. I imagine the Bishops are studying this as they study no other problem of our day.

Essentially it rises from the feeling that the wisdom of the world has developed faster than the Church's doctrines, that there is no chance whatever of modern man accepting them, and that the only hope lies in a ruthless pruning of beliefs which had their use at an earlier stage of man's development, but have come to be actual obstacles in the way of such a spiritual religious flowering as mankind has never known. Like Paul they would "put away the things of a child"— and these "things" include a lot of Paul! Why do Catholics who think like this remain in the Church? The reasons vary from man to man. But I think that upon most the Church still retains a hold stronger and deeper than they can analyze; they feel, or half-feel, that there is some link with Christ which would be broken if they left her. They

were in the Church by divine grace, and the hold
of grace is not soon (or perhaps ever in this life
totally) broken.

The acceptance of the world's wisdom as the
standard by which the teaching of divine revelation
is to be judged, while it is an abiding temptation
for the Christian, is a long way from the mind of
Christ. There is a right use of the world's wisdom,
there is a refusal of adulthood in not using it, but
there is a danger in it always. The official name
of the danger is secularism. Protestants are in that
danger, and so are Catholics. If it spreads, Ecumenism is at a standstill. For Ecumenism means as a
minimum that we should draw closer. Closer to
what? We must see what light we can get on
secularism as a peril to ourselves.

2

Atheism and secularism are clear ideas with a long
ancestry. We know what they mean. At least we
did, until yesterday. But now their clearness is
being muddied; Christians have moved in on them.
The old-line atheist has a genuine grievance when
a Catholic priest in good standing writes urging
atheism, and another (in rather less good standing)
says that Jehovah was the first atheist. The one
may, of course, have been merely indulging in a
flourish of heels, the other may have been working
on the principle that the best way to get attention
is to startle.

But some of today's Christian spokesmen, the
ones who get the headlines, are not just trying to
startle: theirs is no gimmick. The simple fact is
that the line between religion and atheism (the

denial of God) has been badly smudged; that between religion and secularism (the exclusion from consideration of any world but this) can hardly be seen at all. All this began outside the Catholic body; it is now to be met inside. To understand what is happening to ourselves, we must look at it.

The fading of God from the minds of believers had at first no element whatsoever of rejection. It was a following of the line of least effort. It was all very well for Shirley to write:

> The glories of our blood and state
> Are shadows, not substantial things.

The trouble is they look substantial. It is the spiritual that looks shadowy. It is not easy for men's minds to cope with; it doesn't force itself on our attention as the material order does; it calls for the use of mental muscles that the daily running of life never needs at all. Men who would have died rather than deny God did not use their minds upon Him, did not in that sense make Him their own. There was reverence, but no continuing awareness: to the word "God" less and less actual meaning attached.

For many sincerely religious people God was a kind of non-luminous cloud on the horizon of their religion; for a God so little comprehended, what function was there? Decisions of right and wrong, in doctrine and on morals, came to be made quite normally without reference to what He might want. The sense of the supernatural— God intervening, God caring, God commanding, God judging—was not rejected: it simply grew less and less till it was no longer there. I do not mean that this is the whole story of Protestantism in our time. But it is a part. To an outsider it seems a considerable part. Christ's first commandment—to love God with every element of one's being—no longer had any sufficient reality to grip on. Religion came to concentrate everything on love of neighbor, or rather service of neighbor, here on earth—a life to come not denied, but not adverted to, save in funeral services. This is secularism-in-practice, not aware of itself as secularism, but giving all mind and all effort exclusively to this world—with God and the other world, even when believed in, making no discoverable difference.

From God inactive to God dead was an easy step and by a handful it has been taken. There is none of the bitterness of classical atheism. For it too is not a rejection of belief, but more a shedding, like the taking off of a garment not needed in the climate in which we now are. Not only, it is claimed, can we handle our problems without God, we can handle them better without Him—belief in Him is an actual hindrance to the building of that perfect human order which is man's real business.

In this secularist assertion of man's real business they link not only with Marxist atheism but with the Christianity we have been considering. And Catholics are drawn toward it in increasing numbers. For good or ill? Or for a mixture of both?

We are to love our neighbor as ourself, says our Lord. That seemed to demand that we love ourselves a lot—if we love ourselves only meagerly, then that's how we shall love our neighbor. Yet self-love can be a greater root of evil than love of money:

indeed love of money has its own roots in love of self, as have nine-tenths of the evils that afflict mankind.

Consider another text: "God so loved the world that He gave His only begotten Son." If God loved the world, then we must love it. And how do you distinguish loving the world from worldliness? The plain truth is that the world can distract us, obscuring realities mightier than itself; it can ruin us, winning us wholly to itself. Yet we must love it because God loves it: we must understand it, develop its possibilities, because God has committed it to us. Yet we must not become worldly!

The world's peril to man's soul has occupied more of the Church's mind than man's duty of developing the world's possibilities, especially as they concern humanity's life in the world. The sufferings of the individual she has indeed taken into account—with hospitals, orphanages, houses for the aged, homes for the insane. But the improvement of the whole condition of humanity, a movement toward an ideal human society here upon earth, has not been through the ages a notable part of her message, any more than of Christ's message as the Gospels tell it.

That, of course, is the goal of mankind as seen by the Secularist, though not by him alone. William Blake was no Secularist who wrote:

> I will not cease from mental fight
> Nor shall my sword sleep in my hand
> Till we have built Jerusalem
> In England's green and pleasant land.

Now more and more Christians see it so, more

and more Catholics. And for Catholics there is a danger that is worth analyzing.

In the new Catholic excitement over the ideal society to be built by men in this world, there is a real turning away, a literal aversion, from the next; one can hear in Catholic voices irritation at any mention of what used to be called the spiritual life, of revelation, of eternity, as though these were not only irrelevant, or at best marginal, but an actual distraction from man's main task. It is as if one had to make a choice between believing in the next world and serving men in this—very much as the atheist taunts the Church with offering "pie in the sky" instead of fighting poverty here. But both worlds are real and one must live mentally in both.

Is the building of an ideal human society here on earth the goal of Christian men? It is *a* goal certainly, but it cannot possibly be *the* goal, and for a reason which means nothing to the Secularist, but must at least give a Christian pause. The reason is that it excludes the overwhelming majority of the human race, the countless myriads of the dead. And Christ died for all men; and all who have not refused Him by self-love grown monstrous will be in His kingdom. So says the Council (*The Church* 2).

Plato's Republic, More's Utopia, William Morris's Nowhere, Samuel Butler's Erewhon, Blake's Jerusalem, Marx's Classless Society—each begins with men actually living and serves men still to be born—serves them, that is, for the space of their life on earth; it can't do anything for them after that. However perfect it may be, the society men build here is still temporary, a hostelry, not an abiding place. It is our Christian duty to work for its creating and perfecting. But it is not the ultimate goal: how could it be when the majority of the human race is barred from it and those who do reach it cannot stay long in it?

3

Are the men of today, using purely human resources, any likelier than their ancestors to bring the Ideal Society into existence? We talk too easily of human progress, treating scientific and technological growth as if it meant a progress in man himself.

Reading the Old Testament or Egypt's hieroglyphs or Babylon's clay tablets, reading Sophocles and Euripides, or Plautus and Terence, or Herodotus or Tacitus, we meet our own kind of men and women; the thrusting self that is so strong in them is not notably diminished in us. When we come upon Bonhoeffer's statement that man has come of age, we can but think what a coming-of-age party he had—millions dead in Hitler's gas chambers, ten thousand Polish officers murdered in Katyn Wood, hundreds of thousands destroyed in a couple of flashes at Hiroshima and Nagasaki. The Council seems more realistic: "The whole human family has reached an hour of supreme crisis in its advance towards maturity" (*Church and Modern World* 77).

But even if the human race—or some of it!—has at last reached a maturity denied to our ancestors, the questions stands: Are human resources adequate for the earthly society we dream of? Or is God's revelation—of why men are here and where life leads—necessary to be known and brought into action?

If you frequent too many Catholic conferences you might get the feeling that our clerical and academic spokesmen have given up all expectation of building our relation to God into the very texture of life; at best they hope it will not wholly vanish from the Catholic consciousness but will survive as an extra which people have decided not to give up. Meanwhile *the* religious task is the improvement of man's social-political condition here on earth.

There is a lack of sophistication about this. Social *planning* raises questions to which only God can supply the answer; and social *building* has to contend with damaged elements in man which only God can repair. We'll look at the building problem first.

Leon Trotsky said, as against belief in another world, "We declare that we mean to create for the human race a real paradise upon earth." That was fifty years ago. But Trotsky's "we" included Stalin, and Trotsky died in exile, killed with an axe. Bukharin, a most attractive early Soviet philosopher, wrote in *Pravda*: "Christian love, embracing all, even the enemy, is the worst adversary of Communism." It was not Christian love that put Stalin's bullet in Bukharin's brain.

I mention these two not as an argument against Communism, but as a reminder of one vast difficulty in the way of any human order. From the beginning until now the principal source of social evil has been self-interest, self-assertion. Not one of us is free of it. It may vary from a general decency flecked with small selfishness to a monstrous selfishness relieved by an occasional flicker of decency. And no social order is not damaged by it—nor is the Church an exception.

Improving the social system will not heal the disease in the citizens; as the cliché has it, no skill in cookery can make a good omelette out of bad eggs. Improving the system will not make bad men good, weak men strong, greedy men moderate, arrogant men co-operative, vain men sane. Men have shown that in an emergency they can rise above their level; but in the daily run of life, self will constantly threaten to dominate.

Only one way of healing has been found: Christ's command that we have for our neighbor the same kind of love that we have for ourself, with its incredible postscript: "Love your enemies, do good to them that hate you." Unrealistic? It is not an easy rule, certainly, to live up to; even saints have never found it so. But no other rule even promises results: if this one is unworkable, then the disease of self is incurable. But it is not unworkable, as men have shown through the centuries. Even to make the effort to live by it, with howsoever many failures, changes a man.

The problem is to get ourselves to make the effort, given that it puts so great a strain upon habit and instinct. With Christ helping, it is possible. Knowing Him for what He is, we accept the rule. He did not simply pull it out of the air; it was the expression of life as He knew it to be, as He lived it. He was ever conscious of His heavenly Father: so must men be if they are to live by His rule of life. He saw this life as a road, a way, to another. "I go to prepare a place for you": men must see it so, too. We must be prepared, as He was, to lose leg or hand or eye here on earth in order "to enter into life" (Mk 9:43–48). Only with Him living in us shall we have the strength for the effort His kind of life demands of us.

Obviously, if a man does not believe in Christ all this is idle talk: he must simply make the best of things as he finds them. But to believe in Him and to confine that belief to our own personal life, to think that the life of men in society can be conducted without reference to Himself or His Father or the world to come, without drawing on the vital energies He offers men—this I find incomprehensible.

We must work for a better order of society, and work for it with men who do not share our beliefs. But we should never forget that, until they *do* come to share them, the difficulties in the way of a healthy social order arising from the disease of self lack any sure treatment.

Yet even with men wholly (and improbably) healed of that disease, a social order raises questions which selflessness alone cannot answer; some of them only God can.

You remember the epigram of Voltaire's friend Condorcet, that Religion began with the duplicity of the first knave and the simplicity of the first fool. Like all epigrams it leaves out too much. But what truth there is in it applies not to religion only but to all earthly systems—they must all cope with the duplicity of the knaves and the simplicity of the fools.

The knaves will set their cleverness to work to twist the most perfect system to serve their own interests by exploiting the fools: and of course the fools—you and I—have our own duplicities, our own dashes of knavery. The first fact of sociology is that any system must be built of damaged material —human beings, that is.

I have already mentioned that my father was a devotee of Karl Marx and that throughout my boyhood every meal meant a monologue on Marxism—the theme being that the present system was all that needed improving. By the time I was twelve I saw that this was not true. Men need improving too, and radically—and improving the system will not be enough. The Council notes the tragic fact of "man painfully searching for a better world, not working with equal zeal for the betterment of his own spirit" (*Church Today* 4). Never trust any social reformer, of the Right or Left, who talks only of his system, and does not face the problem of the men of whom it must be built and by whom it must be conducted.

In the practical order the vital problem for the social-political thinker is how to heal the disease of self from which no one of us is wholly free: hardly any such thinkers discuss it in depth. There is healing in Christ our Lord—in His two commands to love God and neighbor, in the life He will pour into us if we will let Him. In that lies the greatest, though not the only, service that religion must continue to offer society.

But even with ideal citizens, with self-interest wholly mastered, an ideal social order cannot be guaranteed. For there must still be agreement as to what constitutes an ideal social order, and mere selflessness will not produce that. Honorable men may honorably differ about it, differ even to bloodshed.

In Queen Victoria's England, Macaulay could write of the Roman Republic's first days:

> Then none was for a party,
> Then all were for the State;
> Then the great man helped the poor,
> And the poor man loved the great.

To a lot of Englishmen then—a majority perhaps —that sounded splendid. To a lot of Englishmen today—a majority? I don't know—it sounds sheerly nauseating. Certainly it would have infuriated another who dwelt at the time in Queen Victoria's England, Karl Marx.

Class differences may seem normal and even valuable to one set of men, abominable to another. Even more fundamental is the distinction between society and its individual members. All sane men value both; but instinct, temperament and upbringing will incline them toward one or the other as primary. The balance is delicate, never perfectly achieved. But serious unbalance can be calamitous.

Too much emphasis on the rights of the individual could move in the direction of anarchy; too much on the rights of society can turn very speedily into tyranny. At present the movement— of Right and Left alike—is away from the individual, and it looks as if it is speeding up. Education is already mainly in the State's hands and no one would bet on schools of the parents' choice being allowed to continue anywhere. The right to life is less absolute than ever, with military conscription everywhere practised. In most countries animals are vivisected for the advancement of medical science; in Hitler's Germany living men were operated on for the same purpose, and the Court which tried one of the doctors for murder could not answer his claim that it was right to cause this suffering to a few individuals for the good of all.

From Government officials urging the poor to use contraception it is not a long step to imposing contraception on them. Indeed if the experts decided that society's health requires a lower birthrate, it would be simple to set a maximum number of children beyond which no family must go. (A year after I wrote that, the suggestion was in fact made by a Cabinet Minister in India.)

Upon what principles can such matters be decided? Preferences and prejudices are not principles, neither are habits and customs. Questions of human rights cannot be answered by a count of votes, still less can questions of morals. Public opinion, with individual or collective self-interest to color it, has endorsed great evils in the past and is no more certain to be right in the future.

The health of society depends upon its rightly understanding the world and men. And it did not make either. Without the mind and will of God who made both, it is doomed to sickness. For the Christian a primary duty is to bring God to the service of society's health. How well are we equipped for that?

3

When the thirties were drawing toward the Second World War, one of England's better-known literary men, Middleton Murry, a close friend of D. H. Lawrence, anticipated the "Death of God" men. He wrote his views under the heading "Goodbye to

God." This amused a Catholic reader, because the word "Goodbye" is a contraction of "God be with you." He noted that Mr. Murry said:

> Somewhat illogically 'Adieu'
> But the bon Dieu says 'Au revoir'—

God responds to his "Goodbye" with "I'll be seeing you."

And that is the answer to all who bow God out. The theory is that mankind, having come of age, must "put away the things of a child"—including belief in God. Men can solve their own problems with their own resources. This has always been the position of the atheist, the secularist. There are Christians, including Catholics, who are coming very close to it: there are secularizers, atheisers, some of them very devout, who do not see God as relevant to the life of man-in-society, who build their own wall of separation between God and the state. And indeed religion has often enough, by its concentration upon the individual soul and the next life and its silence about social evils, almost joined hands with the secularist in his dismissal of religion's essential function in the life of society.

The Vatican Council has answered that—the social shaping of our world is part of our duty to God: "Christ's redemptive work . . . involves also the renewal of the whole temporal order . . . the Church's mission is to penetrate and perfect the temporal sphere with the spirit of the Gospel" (*Laity* 5). "God's plan for the world is that men should work together to restore the temporal sphere of things and develop it unceasingly" (ibid. 7).

This does not mean shifting the emphasis from religion to life. The Council has urged discussion with atheists, and they have light to shed for us. But there is necessary knowledge about men and the world which they simply have not got. With richness of investigation in this area or that, they don't know what life is all about. We are here, you and I. A while ago we were not. Not such a long while before that, nobody was. In a while we shall not be. So what's it all about?

Why is anything here, why isn't there nothing? Why are men here? What comes next? Does anything come next?

No science pretends to answer these questions. There is a whole school of philosophy which insists that they are not even questions. But we still need to know, if we are to handle intelligently the *section* of human life which lies between conception and death. Religion tells us. It is not simply a sideline for those who tastes happen to run that way. It matters, and matters vitally. The question of questions, upon which the health of any society inescapably depends, is what man means to it, how men should be treated, what is their *value*—not for special gifts that this one or that one may have, but *as man*. If there is no mind at the origin of the universe, then men emerge from the bosom of matter for no particular reason, remain suspended a while above it, and after a space are re-merged in it. Seeing men thus, it is hard to see them as valuable. The materialist may hold, on no very clear evidence, that all men are equal; but on those terms they are all equal to nothing much.

A given thinker might decide not to bother about the individual man, and bank everything on the social order, with men as replaceable spare parts in the Collective Machine. Karl Marx was so much in love with his blue-print of the Classless Society that he seems never to have asked whether it would fit man. Lenin did at least see the difficulty, and evaded it: by the time the Classless Society arrived, he said, men would be different! Bernard Shaw took one further step: if men were not adapted to it, nature must produce a creature that would be.

But the believer cannot be as irresponsible as that. Nor need he be. He has it from man's Maker that *every* man is a union of matter and spirit, by his spirit immortal, made in God's image, and that Christ died for him. This is the only view of man which makes man valuable simply for being a man. Society desperately needs such a view. But it cannot have the Christian view of man forced on it. Man must be persuaded of its truth. And this will call for a vast effort by all the Churches. That is the first issue of Ecumenism and the surest test of its reality.

And each Church, ours included, must ask itself the soul-searching question: can its own members spread this view of man? Do they even grasp it?

9

How Living
Is Christ?

1

There is something intensely warming to the heart in the ideal of Ecumenism—but what has it to offer the coolness of the head? In other words, when we strive for ecumenism what are we striving for? What would be gained by a drawing into one all who accept Christ; what will be lost if the Churches stay fragmented as they now are?

A Church is not a society whose function is to make its members happier or even holier, better nourished spiritually, kindlier. It should do all these things, but they are not what it exists for. It is not, we have noted, a service station to which its members come for a re-fill or for repair. *It exists to do work that Christ wants done.* There is His good news to be given to the world, there is the life which He wants men to have more abundantly: quite simply there is Himself to be given to mankind. He has chosen to do this work through men:

it will be done better or worse according to two things: their willingness and their competence.

With Christianity fragmented, Christians are not even agreed as to what the good news is, as to what Christ did for us or what He wants of us. We must come back to this. What is even more depressing is the absence, in the rank and file of us, of knowledge of Christ himself.

I say in the rank and file of us: there are no ways left of mass conversions (if there ever were!): all depends upon the ability of each of us to bring our Lord alive in the people we personally meet. And I cannot feel that we have enough knowledge of Him ourselves: I don't mean theological knowledge—just the elementary knowledge of the man Christ Jesus.

In the Appendix there is an examination I have given to crowds, Catholic and Protestant, at all educational levels, all over the English-speaking world. They answer the questions and mark the answers in their minds. My experience as an "examiner" tells me that Christians generally do not do well on these elementary questions: that is why I wrote *To Know Christ Jesus*. I ask audiences not to tell me their marks—the test is for their information, not mine. But their faces tell all. One occasion I remember well. The audience numbered 3,000. The Monsignor, in the chair, opened his concluding remarks with the words "I have just flunked a test," whereupon 2,900 faces relaxed. After all, if Monsignor didn't pass. . . .

Ecumenism is a splendid goal; each step towards it is good. But our growing interest in our fellow Christians will not get us far if it is accompanied by a diminishing interest in Christ our Lord. Upon the place Christ actually holds in the Christian life as it is lived depends the future not only of Ecumenism, but of each Church, including our own.

Is our interest in Him less than it was?
Superficially, at least, it would seem to be.

Our Fathers in the Faith sang:

> Jesus, the very thought of Thee
> With rapture fills my breast.

We do not talk now of rapture filling our breasts; but, stripped of colorful language, is the experience still ours? We know what Bach made of "Jesu joy of man's desiring": how strong is our desire for Him or our joy in Him? I have not come upon any recently-written hymns that are widely sung, even by Protestants who sing more than we. And indeed there is not much to sing about in the New Theology, as yet anyhow. One can't even say it with any lucidity, much less sing it. (Note to myself: find out if Paul Tillich ever wrote a hymn.)

Our question "Is it the same Church?" might have as a sub-section "Can it sing the same hymns?" And, as will be clear, I'm not thinking of the poetical quality or the wording. After all, people don't sing the love songs their ancestors delighted in, yet they still fall in love. I'm thinking of what the hymns are actually saying. To use a phrase from my son Wilfrid's novel, *The Hack*, could we sing some of our best-known hymns "strapped to a lie-detector"? Every Catholic must answer that question for himself, for the answer depends on what Christ means to us. We should be missing too much if we see Him simply as a "piece" in the pattern of Redemption, building no personal friendships with the Christ who actually was. And is.

Meanwhile what of Christians generally? To many He seems rather like a figure in one of His own parables—the Good Samaritan, say—than a Man who lived and suffered and rejoiced, had kinsfolk and practiced a trade. To many devout Christians Christ is little more than a hallowed name for the aspirations of the human heart.

This seeing of Christ not as a person but as love-of-neighbor personified surely accounts for many who spoke of Gandhi as Christlike, knowing as little of Gandhi as of Christ. In practice it means seeing both of them as one's own best self. And oneself at one's best—even Gandhi at *his* best—is a pathetically and frighteningly impoverished substitute for the Christ of Nazareth, Capharnaum, Bethany and Jerusalem—the Christ who was in the beginning with God, and who was God.

All through our years of teaching the Faith under the open sky we had been meeting a particular line of refusal to be concerned with any enquiry as to Who Christ was or What He was. Such questions were dismissed as mere theology; what mattered was the objector's personal salvation: which reduced the whole great fact of Christ to "What's in it for me?"

The "I'm saved" man was a special type. Now something of the same attitude, altruized into "What's in it for men," is all over the Christian world under the name of relevance. That has suddenly become the Golden Word. Where once a statement about God and man had only to be true to be accepted, now it must be relevant. And

"relevant," with its co-word "meaningful," is applied very narrowly—most of theology is excluded.
Yet every truth we learn about God is a new reason
for loving God—and what could be more relevant,
more meaningful, than that? To love God is Christ's
first commandment. But one hears precious little
talk these days of loving God.

2

Ecumenism means that the Christian Churches have
drawn closer to one another, and want to draw
closer still. The union of minds, which means agreement as to what God wants men to believe, may be
far in the future; but the union of hearts, the realization that one's fellow Christians love God and are
loved by Him, is already in being.

In Chapter 6 the question was considered in
some detail whether the Catholic Church regards
all Christians as members of Christ's Mystical Body.
Here I note a single fact, too often overlooked: that
obviously the answer any man gives *must* be affected
by what the phrase Mystical Body of Christ means
to him; and obviously that depends on what Christ
means to him. By calling these statements "obvious,"
I am swimming against today's stream: emphasis
on "meaning" is mere legalism.

It is a strangeness in our religious world that
words can acquire a kind of consecration, while
their meaning is left for each man to decide as he
thinks best: the *words*—Christian, for instance,
Church, grace, revelation—seem to be the substance:
provided we concede *them,* Christian fellowship
is secure. "Mystical Body" is in that category. Is
Christ?

One gets weary of swimming against the stream, yet for the life of me I cannot see how we can discuss Christ's Mystical Body without discussing Himself—Mystical Body of Whom? Mystical Body of What? There is a Catholic answer to both questions —what the Church, living by God's revelation and meditating on it, has thus far seen clearly enough to formulate. What Pope and Council hold we can know. But what do other Churches hold?

We are in difficulty here. There are Protestant voices uttering brilliant thinking; but there is no one to say what Protestantism teaches, or any of the great Protestant Churches; there is no one even to synthesize or summarize or arrange in any graspable shape what any dozen leading Protestant thinkers hold. From a mass of reading, I get an impression at once of richness and vagueness—I feel the richness, but I find it hard to tell myself what the writers are saying on any given matter.

This, I think, results from two facts: (1) they are writing for one another, not for the rest of us; (2) they can neither accept the old formulations nor simply abandon them, but must go on confusing us hopelessly by using the same words with a different meaning. They leave us wondering what they mean by God—e.g. "God is dead," "God is what men are to bring to birth"—and what they mean by Christ. It must be close to forty years ago that one of them answered the question "Is Christ God?" with the words "Christ is the index of my concept of the deity." I thought this was the ultimate in obscurity. But it was not. It sounds to the uninitiated like double talk—but we've gone on since then to triple talk, to quadruple talk.

All this is true of the scholars. What of their

Churches? (And ours, for that matter.) If Ecumenism is to be a word of power changing the world, each Church must look to itself. Each will serve Ecumenism best by making up its mind what its mind is—about God, about Christ, about Redemption, about the Future, here and hereafter. From that there might emerge a Christian Message which the world could hear. At present when I am at interfaith meetings, I wonder what direction "onward" would signify if they sang the hymn "Onward Christian Soldiers." (I find myself thinking idiotically of the Stephen Leacock character who leaped on a horse and galloped off in all directions.)

At present the tendency is to reduce the whole "meaning" of Christ to the Good News. But unless we know who and what the Christ was who died and rose again—if He did—why does His death matter? If it is only a symbol or an example, what did it effect? Has salvation any meaning? Does it refer to the next life only? Does it refer to the next life at all?

What in fact *is* the Good News to which all is reduced? Can it be told just as well without mentioning Christ? This last is the direction in which the leaders of religious thought seem to be moving —the Gospels demythologized, dekerygmatized, de-Christized.

"Hamlet without the prince" is a standard phrase for leaving out the main point. If "Hamlet" were a Gospel and not a play, the same phrase would describe the advanced scholarship of the moment. And all the Churches are feeling its effect.

3

The key question for Ecumenism is "What think ye of Christ?" But you might read reams of ecumenical discussion without guessing it. Everything else is talked about lengthily—in the most Christian spirit!—but He very little.

At an interfaith meeting, some may think Him the Second Person of the Trinity who, in the humanity He had made His own in Mary's womb, died for our salvation, rose again, and is now in heaven interceding for us (Heb 7:25). Some will deny one phrase or another in that statement. And there will be those present who accept none of it, seeing Christ as a parable-figure, a symbol of certain profound truths for the acceptance of which men were the better. No matter. Provided all the participants speak His name respectfully, the discussion can proceed. *For it is not about Him.*

As I re-read that last sentence I am moved to strike it out, so harsh it seems, so anti-ecumenical I hope other people's experience is different; I can only record my own. From so much of what I read, from so much of what I listen to, I find Christ missing. I cannot escape the feeling that He is thought of as one of those theological extras which Christians can proceed to examine in tranquillity when the more practical matters that separate them have been coped with. But He is not an after-matter: no man comes to the Father save by Him. He is the foundation (and what is more practical than a foundation?). Unless we can come to agreement about Christ our Lord—who He was, what He was, what He did, why He matters—

Ecumenism will perish of its own futility. *Nisi Christus frustra.*

I may be right or wrong about the interfaith atmosphere, but certainly in Christian writing we generally feel the absence—and even in some of the ablest Catholic writing the all-but absence— of Christ as *Teacher,* of truths to be held whether of doctrine or of morals. (I have been reading two books by Catholics on Faith: Christ as Teacher is not mentioned.)

The assumption seems to be that mankind, now come of age, must construct its own version of reality (including God), and its own rules for right living, with no apparent reference to Christ's teaching but only to the example He gave of love and denial of self. His teaching, it is felt and is increasingly being said, belongs to His age. Today's problems are different, and today's wisdom must answer them. Today, we agree, has its own light to bring, and it will be to our loss, and Christ's, if it does not bring it. But today will become yesterday, and the Word of the Lord endures for ever. *Stat crux dum volvitur orbis*—the world revolves, the Cross stands.

The Cross indeed is one element in His teaching which has almost vanished—I mean not only the Cross on which He died but the Cross on which, as He tells us, we all of us must die, must die to self daily. There is a distortedness in each of us that only the Cross, our own individual Cross, can straighten.

When St. Aloysius said, "I am a piece of twisted iron, I entered religion to be twisted straight," he was talking of his entry into the Society of

Jesus. But it utters a prime law of the religion of Jesus, and all Christians are called to it.

Suffering is not merely something to be borne courageously, but something to be used, something without which we will not reach our fullness of health or maturity. That truth is not much in today's Christian mind. Well-being here on earth our Lord placed second: "Seek ye first the Kingdom of God, and all these things shall be added unto you." One could easily get the impression that for many a Christian "all these things" *are* the Kingdom of God. Everyone remembers that St. Paul said, "I live, now not I, but Christ lives in me" (Gal. 2:20). We may not all remember the words which come before those: "I have been crucified with Christ."

"Christ lives in me," says Paul. Christ living and operative in the world now, even more than Christ teaching in Palestine long ago, must be at the very centre of ecumenical discussion. For it is the whole point of Christianity. It contains in itself the whole meaning of the Church.

10

The Crisis
of Faith

There is a crisis of Faith now, a crisis of obedience
too—how widespread, there are no statistics to
tell, but wide enough to be frightening. It has two
main roots—disillusion with the Church's leaders
and a questioning of the Church's teachings. We
must glance at each.

1

The Church is in the world, coping with the world.
In the daily running of the Church, Popes have
had to apply the original revelation to human situations, and the application has varied from time to
time, from Pope to Pope. In 1588, as we have noted,
Sixtus v made death the penalty for the use of
contraceptives; a couple of years later his successor,
Gregory xiv, abolished the law. Both were con-
scientious men, holding the same revelation, but
seeing differently the human situation. So with
Innocent iv, who around 1250 introduced torture
into the procedure of the Inquisition, and Nicholas i,
who four centuries earlier had declared torture con-

183

trary to all laws, human and divine. And now the Council has issued the Declaration on Religious Liberty, ending the whole subjection of religious belief to compulsion. As we have noted before, no one blames the mediaeval theologian for not knowing modern physics: neither must he be blamed for not knowing modern psychology.

In nineteen hundred years there have been all sorts of Popes; good men doing their best according to the light they had, but slack and slovenly Popes too, kindly Popes, cruel Popes, wavering Popes, aggressive Popes. But the revelation entrusted to the Church has been preserved and developed (the development might have proceeded faster, some feel!), the Mass has been offered and the sacraments administered, and if the Church had done nothing else that would have been to countless millions a service beyond price. But depending on whether Popes and hierarchies have acted wisely or unwisely, well or evilly, in the daily running of the Church, the face of Christ has been shown to the world clear or dim, the true face or a distortion.

That was the risk He took when He chose to continue His work in the world through a society of men. Not only Popes, but every one of us can further or hinder the work Christ is doing in and through His Body: but Popes in a special way; their reach is wider. Even well-intentioned Popes like Innocent IV and Clement V and Leo X have damaged His work and obscured His face as many a worse Pope never did.

Our reaction to this unhappy fact will vary according to our understanding of the Church. The Pope can loom too large, and a given Catholic may feel that the defects of a given Pope call in question the reality of the Church. But the Church is the Body Christ willed to have, the Pope simply an element in its anatomy and physiology so to speak, an element which may be healthy or diseased. Christ is the whole point.

Seeing the Church so, St. Thomas More chose to die by the axe for his belief that the Pope's supremacy was of divine foundation. And the Pope under whom he came to that decision was the wavering, unreliable Clement VII. Paul VI shines in comparison. But, as Thomas More knew, belief in Papal supremacy was not belief in Clement VII but in Christ: as my belief in Papal Infallibility is not belief in Paul VI but in Christ: as my belief that I received supernatural life in Baptism is not belief in the priest who baptized me but in Christ.

When Peter's successors reach a point of unattractiveness, one might be tempted to leave them in search of better pastors, better pastures. But Peter himself has left us the formula: "To whom shall we go?" What he said of Christ there in Galilee is true of Christ living in His Church: "Thus hast the words of eternal life." However ill He may be served by His representatives on earth at any given moment, He sees to it that in the Church His gifts of truth, and life, and union with Himself are available to us with a fullness and a certainty to be found nowhere else.

These thoughts have been set moving by the account a leading English theologian gives of so much that troubled him in the years before he decided to leave the Church. I talk of it because it troubles so many who still live on unhappily in the Church. The Church is, among other things, a society of human beings with a work to do in the world: therefore it must have officials and sooner or later officials get on your nerves. There is no way out of that. But there have been times when the thing went far beyond this, times when Pope and Cardinals have behaved appallingly. The present episode, with the correspondence growing out of it, shows that there are Catholics who believe that we are now living in such a time. Pope Paul is accused of lying, of "callous dishonesty", for saying that the mind of the Church is not in doubt about contraception. I hasten to say that I do not join in the accusation; "the mind of the Church" does not mean the opinion of Catholics at any given moment, even the present. But supposing I did, or supposing I lived under one of the most evil Popes the Church has known, what then?

My immediate comment is that nothing a Pope could do would make me wish to leave the Church —I can imagine wishing that the Pope would! The thought of leaving on account of it would simply not occur to me; it would be wholly irrelevant. Converts do not enter the Church to gain the Pope, but Christ. Our membership in the Church does not mean union with him, but with Christ. For his failures the Pope is not answerable to me but to Christ. I might weep to see how ill he is serving our Lord: but upon that matter we all have some weeping of our own to do.

Some of those who joined in the discussion spoke of the daily anguish of being in the Church as it is now governed. One spoke of being able to keep going only by a species of "double-think." Personally I am conscious neither of double-think nor of this special anguish.

As to the first, I have never been called upon

to say anything I didn't think, or to hold anything I don't hold. I am called upon to fool neither myself nor anyone else. I shall come back to this.

As to anguish, that is not my state: I love being a Catholic and would love everybody to be. In an article in *Cross Currents,* Spring, 1951, Karl Rahner expressed my own mind with clinical precision: "This Church in her concreteness is *the* Church, the unique Church, the Church of God and of His Christ, the homeland of our souls, the place where we find the living God of grace and of eternal salvation." In the Church I have the great truths about God and man and the God-man; about the goal of life and the way to the goal; a sense of oneness in the Faith with my fellow Catholics. I have Mass and sacraments and the possibility of a union with our Lord to the ultimate limit of my willingness: such anguish as I have is for the millions of my fellow countrymen starved of these things, and for two thousand millions in the world, who, as the Council reminds us, know nothing at all of Christ.

In so far as things are being handled badly, a Catholic can be furious and utter his fury. One remembers St. Catherine of Siena's description of high ecclesiastics—"not men but devils incarnate, blinded by their disordered love of the rottenness of their own bodies." It did not occur to her that the proper reaction was to leave the Church. She stayed on, and helped by prayer and speaking her mind. Free criticism has been for centuries out of fashion, but it has a long and saintly tradition. There will be more opportunity for it in the New Church.

2

But the more serious element of the crisis of Faith is the loss of belief in the truths of revelation. Its roots are in the way the Faith was taught to so many for so long. I could make a horror comic of the things that were taught as Christian Doctrine in one place or another. I once remarked in a lecture that in His Godhead our Lord had no mother, in His manhood no father; and a *teacher* told me I was wrong—the words of the Creed, "He was conceived by the Holy Spirit" meant that the Holy Spirit was His father!

In soil so unpropitious, strange ideas grew as a matter of course. There was the small girl who had been told she must wear a bathing suit in her bath—to spare her guardian angel's modesty; the children who were told that to miss the Children of Mary meeting was like missing Mass; and the small boy who felt that he had sinned by saying a prayer in the toilet (he had worked that one out for himself). I remember a story of two workmen who dared not pick up a nun who fainted in the street—because her body was consecrated!—and who solved the problem by lifting her with their spades. Is this story true or invented? Invented probably, but can we be sure?

Even where the teaching was solidly correct, it was seldom exciting or in any way vitalizing. And where there were two theological opinions, it was normal to teach only one. The young grew up and found that at least some of the beliefs and practices they had been taught with such conviction were wrong: which cast doubt over the rest.

And now, as teachers or as parents, they find the new generation going further into doubt than they themselves ever did. In that sense Ezekiel's words are fulfilled: "The fathers have eaten sour grapes and the children's teeth are set on edge" (for the sense in which God did *not* want the words used, read Ezekiel's eighteenth chapter). The children's doubt often enough forces the parents to face the problem of their own sureness. And meanwhile all about them the word "relevance" is spreading like a fire in dry timber—raising the question of why we should bother at all about doctrines which do not immediately affect us.

The old style teacher of religion might have been only moderately competent. But at least he had no doubts. Today a profound troubling of faith arises from the sense that the teachers are not sure. It is no exaggeration to say that, here and there and elsewhere within the fold, almost every doctrine and practice is being questioned by someone—priest or professor or prominent writer. Some of the questioning is of high value, for too many things have been simply swallowed, too much assumed as Catholic doctrine which simply wasn't. But views are also propounded, unrebuked, which if they should come to be accepted would really mean that it would no longer be the same Church. Quite recently I found myself congratulated *by a Catholic reviewer* on my courage in bringing our Lady *into a book written for Catholics!*

The world is wide, and voices which seem to fill the whole sky for one group are wholly unheard by another; but in some areas certainly, the gap between what is being taught and what the Vatican Council issued in its Declarations is pretty startling. The upshot is, that for great numbers, the virtue of Faith is in a strange condition.

As Hilaire Belloc said, "There's great psychological value in a strong affirmation"; supported by it, masses of people lived their Catholic lives, not very vitally all of them, not very heroically, but with no questioning and with solid spiritual growth—growth, that is, in love of God and their neighbor. But suddenly they think they find the "strong affirmation" wavering. An issue arises in which they must stand up and be counted: and they discover that they are not sure what their number is!

I have only my own experience to go on—what I have seen, what I have heard. But my impression is strong that loss of faith is at once more total and less painful in younger Catholics. What we have called faith's "evaporation" is commoner in them. The reason lies, perhaps, in the narrowness of their experience. They cannot help seeing the Church as Sister This and Brother That, and at a certain level rejection of these may be almost automatic, involving no tearing up of deep roots. Nor have they had the experience their elders have had of situations when life has tested this or that belief, and gone far to verify it—times when, with anguish maybe, they followed the teaching and came to a certainty of its rightness; times when they acted against it, and came to the same certainty by a different way. For such people there can be no question of letting their faith quietly die: its roots are too many and too deep.

3

The crisis of Faith I have referred to is most acute among boys and girls in their middle and late teens and their early twenties. For a long time now, the Catholic young have been uncertain: again and again, lecturing to them on religion, I have felt their cynicism, their eyes saying clearly, "What's his racket?" It was a strain for great numbers of them to believe even while their teachers were agreed and confident: when that agreement broke, and the confidence with it, great numbers of their pupils simply relaxed and let go. It was not exactly rejection; it was more like evaporation. It seemed to be happening all over the place at once: teachers tell one another of it; parents tell *me* of it, thinking I may have the remedy. But no remedy suggests itself. If these young ones had specific objections, we could discuss them. But it isn't like that. Simply something has gone dead in them.

It happened in the past, of course, but never on this scale. The French writer, Henri Ghéon, is almost a laboratory specimen. When he was fifteen he gazed at the Host as it was elevated and found himself saying with total clarity, total certainty: "You're not there." During the First World War his faith returned, and he went on to create the modern way of writing saints' lives. He no more knew the *why* of his faith's resurrection than of its death.

What the hierarchy makes of the phenomenon of evaporation, I don't know. The Council Documents, I think, do not mention it. Nor have I met it in Encyclicals or Pastorals. I once poured out

my fears about it to a high ecclesiastic. He listened
politely. When I'd finished, he said: "Yes, indeed."

If we open the question with the young themselves, they also listen politely. They know we are
doing what we think to be our duty; they are kind
to our immaturity. *They feel they've had it all already.* Unless we can break through that, we haven't
a hope of getting anywhere with them.

Something has gone wrong with their religious
growth. In many instances even the doctrines are
ill taught; sometimes ignorantly, with their meaning unrecognizable; often woodenly, as formulas
never related to the life in themselves or in the
pupil. But even where they are taught well, the
essential may have been missed. You can tell this if
you talk to them of Christ. You find that they have
had Him too. He has evaporated with the rest. Had
theirs been a living relation, He could not simply
have evaporated. Teaching alone will not produce
this; there must be response. But how respond to
what is barely taught? Christ's presence in the
Eucharist is cast in doubt by His absence from the
class-room.

4

I have called the loss of agreement and of confidence sudden. So recently a boy could lose marks
for saying "the Trinity" instead of "the Blessed
Trinity"; so recently one master known to me could
say to his class "If any boy has no devotion to our
Lady, I'll beat it into him." And now so many
teachers regard our Lady and Trinity alike as irrelevant. I have heard some of them urging the
values of scepticism in the young to a point where

one felt they were rewriting the Theological Virtues as Doubt, Hope and Charity.

I am, of course, over-stating. What we are seeing is a reaction against the old cut-and-dried handing out of formulas on Believe-or-lose-your-soul terms, with the students memorizing to satisfy the examiner while their minds were on other matters. What has happened is that the reaction has in some places gone too far—reactions usually do, to begin with. A balance must be found. It had better be soon.

The truth is, I think, that teachers of the Faith (in school or pulpit) had it too easy for too long. God's infallibility clothed the Church and the Church's infallibility clothed them. Their hearers might stop going to Mass and Sacraments, in a proportion which in any other field might have raised a question of the competence of the teachers. But there were two explanations that worked automatically: either an irreligious home or sexual passion. And there were always, thank God, numbers who stayed faithful.

But the new attitude of the young cannot be brushed from consideration like that. Some years ago I wrote a pamphlet with the title "Are We Really Teaching Religion?" What I have been describing may be part of the answer to that impolite question. In the pamphlet I urged that doctrinal teaching in schools must lead to "a personal intimacy with our Lord . . . *everything has to be built upon that.*"

Has it been? My own experience of high school seniors and college students is that while knowledge of the great dogmas varies between very good and miserably bad, precious little is known of our Lord

Himself as He is to be met in the New Testament. Glance at the examination paper in the Appendix: it tests knowledge of Christ as the Gospels show Him living and moving among men. The questions it asks are almost laughably elementary but most of the Catholic students I have met could not get a passing grade on it. Nor could some of their teachers. Which means they do not know the Christ so many of them have already refused or are in danger of refusing. They need Christ desperately. But a Christ hardly more real to them than a figure in one of His own parables cannot vitalize.

What is to be done? There are those who seem to be urging that the troubled Catholic should be taught no more than he can be expected to believe. To this end there is a great restating of revealed doctrines which takes the course of emptying out the mystery, which only too often means emptying out the nourishment. What is left presents no difficulties to the mind, but no stimulation, either, to will or emotions. Men will not die, or even die to self, for a set of maxims, however true, however noble. To reduce Christ's life to the parable of a kind man crucified removes Him from the battle we all have to fight against pride, anger, covetousness, lust, gluttony, envy and sloth. My own experience with half-believers, ex-believers, or unbelievers in the street-corner meetings of the Evidence Guild is that to teach them about the Trinity, and to introduce them to the Christ whose God the Trinity is, can really change minds and lives.

One thing fatal in the teacher is loss of nerve, fear of seeming old-fashioned himself, or wondering what is the minimum he can reasonably expect his pupils to accept. He must give them his all, or rather Christ's all. The teacher, in classroom or pulpit, must try to help them build their relation to God into the very texture of their lives. If he hopes to do no more than persuade them not to let God wholly vanish, to keep Him as an extra they have decided not to let go, then he has not merely lost the war for their Faith, he has not even fought.

11

Sunrise
or Sunset?

I first raised the question with which this book opens—whether we are at a sunrise or a sunset—in newspaper columns. I did not try to answer the question, but there were those who thought that even to have raised it was unduly pessimistic. They pointed to the reception of Pope Paul by the United Nations, the new friendliness of Jews, the five-day love-affair between the Pope and the City of Bombay, the visit to the Vatican of the head of Soviet Russia (one remembers how Stalin flicked aside a proposal that Pius XII be invited to the Peace Conference with a contemptuous "How many divisions has he?"). All this is not merely splendiferous, but splendid. Yet splendor can go as well with sunset as with sunrise: remember Francis Thompson's line to the Sun: "Thou dost thy dying so triumphally." That the outside world is reacting newly is not the test. What is happening inside the Church?

1

What is happening inside the Church? We are not concerned with the great dogmas which give us the structure of Reality—God and Christ and Grace and the World to Come—but with her own structure as a pilgrim Church upon earth, with her relation to other religious bodies and to the human race as a whole.

Structurally there have been great changes. There is a new balance between the Curia and the Bishops. From the beginning of the Council this was made to seem the main issue—the Curia was a sinister body of faceless men and everything depended on its defeat. In fact, the Curia is simply a Cabinet through which the Pope administers his immeasurably complex functions as Head of a world-wide Church. He would be as crippled without a Cabinet as would the President of the United States or Britain's Prime Minister. Cabinets are composed of men: some fulfill their tasks better than others. But unless the Pope is to do everything himself—or leave practically everything undone—a Cabinet he must have.

There is indeed a conflict, a genuine conflict of minds, about the relation between the Curia, *through* which the Pope works, and the Bishops of the world-wide Church *with* whom the Pope works. By the very nature of the case, the men on the spot day in day out tend to exercise more control over more things; that is a problem of bureaucracy. It seems clear that the proportion between Curia and Episcopate had come to need considerable correcting. This has begun: at the one end, Curial Cardinals are now appointed for five years and not for life, and go out of office on the death of the Pope who appointed them. At the other end, we have seen the reassertion of the "collegiality" of Bishops; and the Senate, or Synod, of Bishops to confer regularly with the Pope is past the blue-print stage.

A certain amount of confusion cannot but be there, with the old order not dead, the new not established. We *still* read of some rather old-style interventions by the Curia. Are these the death throes of an institution unable to believe that death is upon it, or are they signs that it is now returning to full (and nefarious) life? So sure are some Catholics that the latter is the explanation that they were almost disappointed when Pope Paul reversed a Curial veto on Catholics going to a Protestant Church in Rome to pray for reunion. But we have had other signs of change—a protest by many bishops over some Curial instructions on Church music, which would once have been accepted meekly, in public at any rate; and a response from the French hierarchy which was in effect a rejection of a Curial schema for a theological investigation of the French Church.

Whichever way this particular matter goes, it will not mean that we have another Church taking the place of the one we grew up in. After all, Cardinals as we now know them are not of the essence; they were not there for the first thousand years. Nor is the present centralization of the essence. It looks as if national hierarchies are to have more freedom of decision in their own areas. This is a recognition of a profound value in national differences: "each nation develops the ability to express Christ's message in its own way" (*The Church in the Modern World,* 44). We may yet see startling changes beyond any that have yet happened in the Church's way of conducting her life and of ordering her resources for the attainment of her single intention: "that God's Kingdom may come, and that the salvation of the whole human race may come to pass" (ibid. 45).

There will be a wilderness of ideas propounded to this end, and fierce differences among good men. Without a guiding authority the end might be a wilderness. That is why Christ put Peter there.

All this is for the future, perhaps a near future. But we already have a notable restructuring of the Church. The senate, or synod, of Bishops to confer regularly with the Pope has had its first meeting. The Federation of Priests in Chicago is a sign of a new relation between the clergy and their own bishop. Parish Councils, largely lay, threaten the absolutism of one of the world's most entrenched monarchies. An intelligent modernization of the structure has at least begun. But how many will still be there to enjoy the modern conveniences?

Too many of the tenants have moved out or are thinking of moving. If only the restructuring had happened earlier, we may mournfully observe—very much as we now say "If only the Council of Trent had preceded the Reformation, the Church might not have lost the North of Europe"; or "If only *Rerum Novarum* had come forty years before the Communist Manifesto instead of forty years after, the Church might not have lost the working class"; or "If only the Declaration of Religious Liberty had come while the Church still had power . . ."

2

Nineteen centuries after Christ the majority of the human race—"two thousand million human beings" the Council said—has *not* been taught Christ's Gospel. The minority, which *has* been taught, does not always stay taught. We must face the sobering realization that the Church has simply not done what Christ founded it to do. Has it been a failure? A bitter word, that. Certainly it has not been a very notable success. Whose fault? It is not for me to answer. But at least we can lose nothing by examining the possibility that some of the fault may be ours.

'Tis not in mortals to command success,
But we'll do more, Sempronius, we'll deserve it.

Have we deserved it?

By one test we certainly have not: there has been no mobilization of all the resources of the Church for so vast a work as the winning of the world to Christ. I say nothing of the scores of thousands of the parish clergy, not very much consulted through the ages, not as such represented at Vatican II. But certainly in the millions of the laity never adequately counted there is intelligence and experience of life, both natural and supernatural, which our leaders could draw on and be the stronger for. And for this no procedures had ever been set up.

The emergence of the laity may prove to be the outstanding difference between the Church of today and the Church before Pope John. The

Council said that the Church's salvific work was to be done not by the hierarchy alone but by the whole Church. It would be hard to find anything like that said by Pope and Council in all the Church's history. We are a long way from Pius IX, with his weeping over Newman's view that the laity should be consulted in matters of doctrine.

We have already discussed the priesthood of the Laity. The apostolate of the Laity is a natural consequence. "They are made sharers in the priestly, *prophetic,* and kingly functions of Christ" (*The Church* 31). "Through baptism and confirmation all are commissioned to a participation in the saving mission of the Church . . . the laity are called in a special way to make the Church present and operative in those places and circumstances where *only through them can she become the salt of the earth*" (ibid. 32). In other words "The head cannot say to the foot, I have no need of you" (1 Cor 12:21), which is what the visible head of the Church seemed to be saying for so many a century. The italics are mine: surely no layman can say those words without shouting them or singing them.

What do the laity make of their new importance? Most, perhaps, give small thought to it. The minority who rejoice at it are not yet at home in it. There is a strange combination of refusing obedience and refusing independence—at once questioning the right of the authorities to give orders in their own sphere, and accusing them of not being sufficiently active in the layman's.

Pause on this a second. There is a kind of almost whimpering complaint—natural enough, perhaps, after centuries of accepting their own insignificance —that the Pope does not take the lead in social and political reform. But this is the civil sphere, the laity's sphere. If Catholic laymen, formed by Christ, indwelt by the Holy Spirit, nourished by revelation and sacrament, and gospel-soaked, gave themselves to the remaking of the world, then the face of the world would really be renewed. The clergy give us the revelation and the sacraments: that is what the Apostles were appointed for. If we demand that they should also be telling us how to run the social order, then an umbilical cord still ties us unnaturally to Mother Church.

But, apart from this, the attitude to authority is highly non-umbilical. The old acceptance is pretty badly frayed. Catholic editors tell the Pope where he is wrong; seminarians picket their bishop; in Westminster Cathedral there was a "pray-in" to protest a friar's removal from editorship by the Master-General of his Order. Laymen are taking their own line about contraception as affecting themselves, and about divorce laws and abortion laws for others. For some of the most articulate Catholics "Mother knows best" is now out as a rule of life.

Much of this is merely the spread of an attitude which has always been normal at the top of society. From the rulers of Catholic nations, Popes could count upon only occasional conformity with their wishes. Except upon dogma and the moral law, rulers made their own judgements and took their own line, flipping aside excommunication and interdict as no more than occupational hazards.

This attitude, normal with monarchs, is now appearing at all levels. But there are two differences.

Dogma and the moral law are no longer sacrosanct; excommunication and interdict are no longer normal weapons. To the interested onlooker, laity and clergy alike seem to be getting away with murder. We have noted that the words "anathema" and "heretic" are not in the Council Documents. There is a new mildness in all Roman pronouncements. This mildness surely reached a high point in the comment on an English priest who left the Church and married, accusing the Pope of callous lying: the *Osservatore Romano* used no such language in answer—it regretted his departure but said that he must follow his conscience.

Dogma and the moral law, I say, are no longer sacrosanct; in morals, particularly, great numbers of Catholics are going ahead on their own with no sense of guilt.

An Archbishop has just joined the growing number who think that Catholics should let their own conscience decide about mixed marriages, contraception and abortion. We have already discussed this. Upon sin, especially upon sexual sin, men's judgement is only too easily a mask for their desire. Many of those who want no talk of law in the moral sphere seem to have a kind of innocence, not knowing sin as Chesterton described it: "powerful as a cannonball, enchanting as a song." In this sphere a sane man knows he cannot trust his own judgement.

The Church will continue to teach with total clarity, as Christ did, what things are sinful. But it may well be that there will be more teaching and urging than commanding. There may be less strict exclusion of sinners from the sacraments. Needless to say, the Roman Curia did not invent this strictness! Paul told the Corinthians to expel from their company a man guilty of incest. Christ gave the Church authority to teach the moral law, and she must teach it. But what she does about disobedience is to be judged by its spiritual effectiveness; it can change with the times. In the world as it now is, the Church may come to feel that men will be brought closer to God by receiving the sacraments than by being denied them.

Pope John said it in the speech with which he opened the Council: "Nowadays the spouse of Christ prefers to make use of the medicine of mercy rather than that of severity. She meets the needs of the present day by demonstrating the validity of her teaching rather than by condemnations." Some old-style Catholics may find mildness to this degree unreasonable. Yet even they must feel that harshness has not much fruit to show. If authority had gone on reasoning with Nestorius instead of condemning him, orthodoxy need not have suffered, and the Church would not have lost so much of Asia.

For a Catholic not well instructed in Theology and Church History, this is a tough time. Every week he is dazzled by some sparklet of the New Theology, never having been properly taught the Old. Brought up in a stable Church, he looks out on a landscape which changes while he looks. But how new is the New Theology? How new, indeed, is newness? And what constitutes stability?

I remember an experience of my own. In the mid-twenties of this century a priest wrote an article in a theological review about the Priesthood of the Laity. By the command of the hierarchy of his country the whole issue was called in and destroyed.

Ten years later we published a book by the same writer and were thought dangerously *avant garde*. And now the Priesthood of the Laity is seen by the Ecumenical Council as a dynamic principle of renewal.

A different example: the Council has said that members of the Orthodox Churches of the East may receive our sacraments and we theirs in certain circumstances. This means that we should be receiving absolution, and Christ's body, and sacramental anointing from men who do not accept Papal infallibility or even supremacy. New and revolutionary? Not at all. Up to the fifteenth century it had been the custom for close to a thousand years.

From the beginning, doctrine has known developments as the revelation given by Christ was lived, thought about and fought about; as new conditions arose to which it must be applied; as the whole human condition was seen more profoundly. And at every stage there were those who saw as betrayals the newer, richer statements to which the Church had given, or would give, her sanction as she brought God's revelation to action in a changing human situation.

Consider this last. There are accidental changes —as when the Roman order collapsed and the barbarian had not developed. When the clergy was the only educated class, all sorts of things had to be done by them if they were to be done at all. With the passage of time some of these things—education, notably—came to seem a clerical privilege, to be clung to at all costs.

But changes are not only accidental. There are profound changes—for the better, generally, though not always—in the order of civilization. Learning advances as the world about us and the past are explored; science advances; philosophy and psychology differ from one age to the next. The graph of civilization and the graph of religion are not the same: they affect each other, of course, but both are liable to long level periods and sudden upswings, and these do not always coincide. The man of the pagan empire, the feudal man, the man of the Renaissance, the man of the space age—to take four—have experienced life and analyzed life very differently.

In the daily running of the Church, Popes can only apply unchanging revelation to the current situation to the best of their understanding of it. Everybody applauded the phrase with which Cardinal Suhard called Catholics to exploration and experiment: "Pioneers must not be blamed for making mistakes." But neither must Popes. In Church or State, as we have noted, the outstanding thinkers *ought* to be ahead of the authorities.

I have called revelation unchanging. There is a possibility of misunderstanding here. In the Church's utterance of the truths entrusted to her, the last word will never be uttered here below—or there above, perhaps. There are two major reasons for this.

First, if I may quote my own *God and the Human Mind*, "No statement either as given in Revelation, or as developed by the Church's living by it, can be more than a beginning. Even if finite words could contain the infinite, finite minds could not extract the infinite from them. But the great definitions proclaimed by the Church as contained in Revelation or issuing from it are light-bearing. And in that light we can grow."

The second reason is of a different sort. Everyone should study carefully Section 44 of the Council's Constitution on the Church in the Modern World for its very close consideration of human experience in the development of theology:

"Thanks to the experience of past ages, the progress of the sciences, and the treasures hidden in the *various forms of human culture,* the nature of man himself is more clearly revealed and new roads to truth are opened. . . . With the help of the Holy Spirit, it is the task of *the entire people of God,* especially pastors and theologians, to hear, distinguish and interpret the many voices of our age. . . . In this way *revealed truth can always be more deeply penetrated.*"

I have italicized three phrases, each saying something that has not always been evident in the Church's practice. I linger on the first: the bringing of various human cultures into the service of the understanding of revelation. As Michael Novak says (in *The Open Church*), "Catholic thought has been too often confined within the conceptual experience of only a part of the human race." We have had splendid examples to the contrary, of course.

St. Augustine brought a new richness into theology from his long study of Plato, dead eight hundred years before him. Eight hundred years after Augustine, St. Thomas drew new and vitalizing concepts from Plato's contemporary, Aristotle. But if the Church had gone east from its Jewish starting point instead of west, the Indian Sankara or the Chinese Lao Tse might have been built into the living teaching of the Church instead of the Greeks. It may still happen. Theologians now in the cradle may some day build them both into a new Christian synthesis to the delight of Augustine and Thomas, perhaps, but to the anguish of many a then-living Thomist or Augustinian.

The possibilities of development are limitless; but so are the possibilities of distortion. To quote *God and the Human Mind* again: "God's desire to be known by us has at all times to cope with the marvelous ingenuity of the questing, discovering, uttering mind of man." A Church with authority to teach in His name, to declare whether the new is also true, is His way of coping. To the man of genius in Theology or Philosophy or Biblical Scholarship, the interventions of authority may seem not only irritating but a roadblock in the way of truth's advance. But Karl Rahner has uttered the fact of it: "The spirit has always held sway in the Church, in ever new ways, always unexpectedly and creatively. . . . He has never abolished authority and laws . . . but again and again brings them to fulfilment in ways other than those expected by the 'bureaucracy'."

Christ's own message is so far beyond what men are prepared for, that, even taught with the utmost clarity, it would not be easily grasped; in a clamor of voices, it can hardly come through at all. Sankara and Lao Tse can only add to the clamor—unless there is a voice speaking with Christ's authority. That is the sense in which authority is opposed not to truth but to chaos.

Anyone who knows of the vast changes made as the centuries passed will not lightly think that what is happening now means the end of the old Church and its replacement by a new. In fact it was a Protestant taunt—in the days when Protestants taunted and we taunted back—that the Church had changed so often and so shamelessly whenever she found it expedient, as to make a mockery of her motto *semper eadem*—always the same. But that was not the Church's motto—it was Queen Elizabeth's, her jesting way of saying that she meant to stay unmarried. Taken seriously, *semper eadem* would not necessarily be a healthy motto; it could mean "in a rut." Changes there must be; the only question is whether the changes develop the identity, or partly submerge it, or destroy it altogether. Nothing in recent decisions of Pope or Council even suggests the last of these. But Pope and Council are not the Church. What will the changes mean to the rest of us?

Our attitude to them will depend on what we see as of the essence. At the conservative extreme there is a tendency to canonize the customary. Thus a French group, the Trumpeters of Jericho, want the Pope and most of the hierarchy excommunicated for heresy. But at the other end there is a kind of dancing delight in change as such, a small-boy pleasure in being the first to tell a wide-eyed audience that they need no longer believe in the Ascension, say, or the souls in Purgatory. I keep being reminded of the beaming face of the lecturer long ago who told us that we had all begun our existence as polymorphous sexual perverts.

That beam is now part of the Catholic landscape. As I have said, I find it hard to think of a doctrine I have not heard denied by a priest. I have grown used to "Surely you don't believe in . . ." Often enough I do. And quite surely. I still have a pleasant companionship, for instance, with certain of the saints, since I live in the certainty that death does not divide (only sin divides). I have no tendency to fall "out of the Ark," no tendency to fall "into the fashion."

But between the grotesque extremes there is a solid movement of the mind; we have all gained by it, and will gain further. Yet we must not pass from swallowing the old to swallowing the new. We lend the experts our ears, but not our minds. For two things especially we must be on the watch.

The first I merely mention here; we have treated of it earlier. It is the central habit of saying *either/or* when we should say *both/and*. In the excitement of an idea new to us, it is easy to discard what we already hold instead of building the two into a fuller truth. We call it the swing of the pendulum—but men are not pendulums.

The second is a sort of sleight-of-hand we practice on ourselves whereby Scripture is quietly slipped under the table. Two instances leap to mind. Those who would escape the traditional teaching on the Real Presence write reams to show all the different things the word "presence" can mean, and seem to feel that all is well if they can hang on to some of them. But Scripture does not use the phrase "Real Presence": it gives Christ's words "This is my body" —and most of the argumentation about "presence" would apply lamely to that.

We have something similar in the statement of some Dutch theologians that the original belief in the Virgin Birth was "not biological." "Virgin Birth" is not a Scriptural phrase. In the Gospels we find Mary's "I know not man" and "Joseph knew not his wife": try to get the words "not biological" into either of these!

The structure planned for the Church by Christ needed mending; it is being mended. All sorts of apparent theological dead-ends have turned out to be invitingly open. But structures and approaches do not vitalize. Only the spirit gives life. All depends on the people of Christ, their understanding of Christ's message, their response to divine grace. Even if His message were to come through more plainly than it has ever come yet, the world will first judge not the message, but the messengers— you and me, in fact. The messengers must live the message they utter.

Consider one point of the message. The only sins we hear Christ actually name as leading to eternal damnation are failures to feed the hungry, to bring drink to the thirsty, clothe the naked, visit the sick. And He gives the reason—failing the needy is failing Him, just as serving them is serving Him: "doing it unto them, you did it unto me." "Feed the man dying of hunger"—Vatican II gives us the quotation—"because if you have not fed him, you have killed him."

Television has brought the world's agonies into our living rooms; but our eyes have not relayed the message to our heart—the art of seeing Christ in all men is not much developed in us. If ever it is, His message will sweep the world.

4

It is the same Church: we have examined some of the differences this sameness embraces! But what lies ahead? Looking at the world to be won, the task seems hopeless. Looking at ourselves, it seems ridiculous. We are so obviously inadequate. But watch that word "obvious."

When I was in Rome during the Council, seeing bishops everywhere, I found myself saying some lines from W. S. Gilbert:

> Bishops in their shovel hats
> Were plentiful as tabby cats—
>   In point of fact too many.

But then I heard two thousand of those bishops singing the Credo in St. Peter's. In that moment, nothing seemed impossible. Mere emotionalism? Watch out for that word too.

Back to "obvious." Certain things seem beyond question. In regard to the world outside, growing more rapidly than the Church is, we hardly act as if we expect to convert it. We are concentrating our efforts on primitive peoples; we seem almost to have given up the civilized.

Are we even holding our own? There is the evaporation of faith in so many of the young, from twelve, say, to forty. No one I meet seems to have any notion what to do about that. And, if public opinion polls are to be trusted, over half the married Catholics of this country are using the Pill. We are still waiting for the Pope's decree: if it both condemns the Pill and forbids the Blessed Eucharist to those who use it, there could be a great falling away—not only the mothers and fathers excluded from the sacraments and effectively outside the Church, but their children not likely to be drawing life from sacraments from which their parents are excluded.

One way or another, a smaller Church seems probable—with far fewer priests and far less money. That would mean a forced withdrawal from the civil order—schools, hospitals, cemeteries. Social services generally will have to be left to those with the resources to handle them. Priests will just have to be priests (at least we shall not see men in Holy Orders teaching algebra to Catholic teenagers, when most of the world knows nothing of Christ our Lord).

There are those—the famous Jesuit, Karl Rahner, is among them—who expect the Church to be everywhere reduced to small groups, with the world no more aware of them than of some of the microscopic sects today. There is a temptation to prophesy —you can't disprove a prophet; you can only live him down. And there is a special temptation to prophesy the worst.

For myself, I make no guess. But there is a certain attitude toward the Church thus reduced which I find hard to understand: the feeling that it really doesn't matter whether the Church is large or small; that there may indeed be more spirituality—more gain to the world therefore—in a Church of obscurity.

This strikes me as more spiritualizing than spiritual, as though the order of secondary causes were of no importance. I long for more and more people, people by the hundred million, to live the Catholic life in the Church. And this is not a worship of bigness: it is just that I cannot sleep comfortably with the thought that millions are starved of food Christ wants them to have, food of truth, food of sacrament. That, I imagine, was why He told His apostles to preach the gospel to every creature. A

Church reduced to a handful could not fulfil that commission very well. The atomized Church which some dream of—each man coming to his own personal conclusion as to God's revelation for men—cannot fulfill it at all.

Fortunately, one clear lesson of history is that the obvious is an unsure guide. It is agonizing even to read of the despair into which the Babylonian captivity, with its destruction of all that they had built over the centuries, plunged the Jews in the sixth century before our Lord. Yet we know that that Catastrophe was the making of the children of Israel. They returned from the captivity a new people.

Pessimism has a way of taking itself for realism. But realism says, "You never know." The Vatican Council may indeed have been a sunset, not a sunrise: there may be a long night before the sun rises again. But, as Claudel phrases it, "The worst is not the surest."

I end with a quotation from Christopher Dawson: "To the observer of the first century A.D. the efforts of the government to solve the economic crisis by a policy of free credit to producers may have seemed infinitely more important than the doings of an obscure handful of fanatics in an upper room in Jerusalem."

The observer would have been wrong. He did not know that the Holy Spirit was in the upper room. When the Church is in question, we must never omit from our calculations the incalculability of the Holy Spirit.

Appendix

THE EXAMINATION REFERRED TO IN CHAPTER 9

One need not be an historian to know where the great things of one's country's history were said and done; if one is English: where William the Conqueror won his battle, where Nelson flew the signal "England expects"; if one is American: where the Pilgrim Fathers landed, where the words "Four score and seven years ago" were uttered. It would be incredible not to know. Apply a similar test to our Lord's life.

1. In what places were the following said or done:
    (a) "Take up thy bed and walk";
    (b) The touching of our Lord's garment by the woman with the issue of blood;
    (c) "Lord, I am not worthy that you should enter under my roof, say but the word ....";
    (d) "Unless you shall eat the flesh of the Son of man and drink his blood, you shall not have life in you."
Allow 10 marks for each answer; as one of these occurred in two different places, the question carries 50 marks.

2. Only once are we actually told that our Lord was joyful. What was He joyful about? (10 marks)

3. Of all the sinners who came thronging around our Lord we are told of only one who actually called himself a sinner (apart from the Penitent Thief, who did not exactly come thronging). Who was he? (10 marks)

4. At the Transfiguration our Lord talked with Moses and Elias. What was the conversation about? (10 marks)

5. To whom did Christ say "I am the resurrection and the life"? (10 marks)

6. We are told in one of the epistles of a virtue Christ learned. What was it? (10 marks)

I find that while Questions 2–6 are admitted as reasonable, the reaction to question 1 varies: those who get full marks think it an excellent question; those who don't know the answers think it pointless and grow indignant—what does it matter *where* these things happened? "Their significance is not geographical," as one candidate remarked.

Of course, the place doesn't matter, any more than it matters where the Pilgrim Fathers landed, or where Lincoln made that incomparable speech, where William defeated Harold, or where Nelson flew his signal. But it *would* be eccentric not to know. If we are really interested in Christ, how could we not know?

ANSWERS

1. All four are told as happening in Capharnaum. "Take up thy bed and walk" was also said at Jerusalem. (An unawareness of the importance

of Capharnaum is a sure sign of no very strong interest in the life Christ lived as a Man among men.)

2. Because God had given the seventy-two disciples insights not given to "the wise and prudent". Lk 10:21.

3. Peter: Lk 5:8. (The publican who said "God be merciful to me a sinner" was a figure in a parable: Lk 18:13.)

4. The death our Lord was to die in Jerusalem: Lk 9:31.

5. Martha: Jn 11:25.

6. Obedience: Heb 5:8.

Index

Aggiornamento, 12
Al-Hallaj, 43
Ambrose, St., 110
Aquinas, St. Thomas, 4, 43, 208
Atheism among Christians, 117, 158-159
Augustine, St., 117, 146, 208-209
Authority:
  of state, 15-16
  in early Church, 2-3, 81
  the point of, 6-7, 10, 16-25, 200, 209
  infallibility, 53-54, 62
  and morals, 27-44, 46, 204-205
  enforcement of, 134, 204
  criticism of, 3-6, 187, 210
  new attitude to, 202-205

Barth, Karl, 29
Bellarmine, Cardinal, 8
Belloc, Hilaire, 151, 190
Benediction, xi
Bigotry, 120-121
Blake, William, 161, 162
Bonhoeffer, 163
Boniface VIII, ix
Browning, Robert, 90, 103
Bukharin, 164

Catherine of Siena, 5, 187
Changes in the Church
  (see also Development of Doctrine), xi, xii, xiv, 11-14, 206-212
  disciplinary, 1-25
  in Mass, 87-88, 90, 98-111

Christ:
  and Caesar, 16, 18
  prayer for unity, 17, 19
  and Mass, 91-98, 103-104
  and the Cross, 181
  and Morals, 30-33
  one Mediator, 147
  sins that will damn, 212
  and ecumenism, 143-145, 173-182
  reality of, 174-177, 180-182
  lack of knowledge of, 72, 174, 193-194, 217-219
  absence from the classroom, 191-194
  and elementary examination, 217-219
  (see also Authority, Changes, Faith, Mystical Body, Papacy)
Church:
  commissioned by Christ, vii, 3, 6
  as teacher, 20-21, 149, 209
  in the New Testament, 1-4, 74-77, 80-82
  and Scripture, 65-83
  and morals, 48-50
  teaching on contraception, 45-64
  pre-Conciliar, viii-x, xi-xii
  post-Conciliar, 198-200
  purpose of, 10-11, 137, 173-174, 187
  infallibility, 51-54, 62
  and the ideal society, 165-167, 170-171

Church: *(Cont.)*
  holiness of, ix-x
  its defects and sinfulness,
    184-187
  has it failed?, 201
  criticised by its members,
    4-5, 187, 210-211
  Catholics who differ,
    155-158, 162
  falling away from, 156,
    185-195, 200
  Karl Rahner on, 187
  what lies ahead, 212-215
Claudel, Paul, 215
Clement V, ix
Communicatio in sacris,
    xii, 13
Condorcet, 166
Conscience, viii, 36-44, 64
Contraception, xiv-xv, 45-
    64, 169, 213
  and the Bible, 55-56
Cremation, 12-13

Dawson, Christopher, 215
Development of Doctrine,
    206-209

Eastern Orthodoxy, 206
Ecumenism, 113-137
  and God, 155-172
  and Christ, 143-145,
    173-182
  and Our Lady, 139-153
  personality problems, 125-
    127, 141, 150, 151-
    152
  soft pedalling, 129, 134
Elizabeth I, 6-8
Eucharist, Blessed, 93-98,
    211
  in both kinds, 105
  reservation and visits,
    97-98

condition for reception,
    108-109, 204-205, 213
Faith:
  crisis of, 152-153, 156-
    158, 183-195
  evaporation of, xiii-xiv,
    63-64, 190-194, 214
Fisher, St. John, 5

Gandhi, 176
Gheon, Henri, 191
Gilbert, W. S., 213
God:
  ecumenism and, 155-172
  "is dead," 158-160, 169-
    170
  fading of, 159-160
  secularism, 159-172

Homosexuality, 56

Immaculate Conception,
    148-149
Imprimatur, 25
Index expurgatorius, 24-25
Innocent III, 7
Innocent IV, 53

John XXII, ix
John XXIII, vii, xiv-xv,
    119, 133, 134, 135,
    205
Joseph, St., 142

Laity, 18-20, 170-171, 201-
    204, 205-206
  priesthood of, 89, 92
Latin, 99-100
Lao Tse, 208-209
Lenin, 172
Leo XIII, 54-55
Life, what it's all about,
    171-172
Liturgy, 101-102

Macaulay, Lord, 168
Mannix, Archbishop, 110
Marx, Karl, 40, 115, 162, 167, 168, 172
Marriage, mixed, 14
Mass (see also Eucharist), 85-92, 98-111
    Obligation, 106-107
Methodism—my experience of, 115 ff.
Morals:
    authority of Church, 27-44, 46, 48-50
    community as general guide, 28-29, 32, 37-38
    love as sole law, 29-32
    situation ethics, 29-30, 33-35, 38
More, St. Thomas, 185
Murry, Middleton, 169-170
Mystical Body, 10, 22
    who are members?, 135-136, 177-178

Nestorius, 205
Nicholas I, on torture, 53
Novak, Michael, 208

Obedience, 18, 73, 82
Our Lady:
    and ecumenism, 139-153
    virginity, 141-142, 211-212
    Assumption, 78, 133, 148-149
    Immaculate Conception, 148-149
    her motherhood of us, 146-147, 150-152
    Catholic exaggerations, 140-141, 145

Papacy, 123-124, 183-187, 207

infallibility, 51-54, 62
Paul, St.:
    and Peter, 4
    and the incestuous Corinthian, 3, 205
    and Nero, 15-16
    and Eucharist, 96
    and Christ, 182
Paul VI:
    on contraception, 58, 61
    on the Mass, 88, 90
    Mysterium Fidei, 93-97
    reverses a veto, 199
Persecution, 53, 81, 183-184
Peter, St., 4, 15-16, 185, 200
Pius V, 6-8
Pius XI, 54
Pius XII, 8
    on rhythm, 60
    Humani Generis, 65
    Mystici Corporis, 135
Prejudice, 120-122
Priesthood, attitudes to, 63
Protestantism (see also Ecumenism), 155-156, 177-178

Rahner, Karl, 187, 209, 214
Relevance, 176-177, 189
Revelation, 20-21, 192
    loss of belief in, 188
    Scripture, xiii, 65-83
    Old Testament, 68-71
    New Testament, 71-83
    Form Criticism, 71-72
    and ecumenism, 77

Sankara, 208-209
Secularism, 159-172, 182
Shaw, Bernard, 172
Sixtus V, 53, 183
Society, the ideal, 160-170

Suhard, Cardinal, 207
Sunrise or Sunset, vii, 153, 197-215

Thompson, Francis, 153-197
Transubstantiation, 94-96
Trotsky, Leon, 164

Utopia, 162

Vatican Council, Second, 17, 27-28, 50, 55
  press coverage of, 63
  what is treated, xiii
  on the Church, 46, 49, 54, 89, 145, 162, 202
  on the Church in the Modern World, 11, 39, 43, 59, 163, 167, 199-200, 208
  on Ecumenism, 18, 135-136
  on the Laity, 170
  on Religious Liberty, 40, 41-42, 43, 53
  on Liturgical Revival, 88, 89

Walewska, Maria, 34-35
Wesley, John, 116, 118